# The Digital Pen

Miriam J Johnson

# The Digital Pen

Navigating the Performance of Authorship
in the Digital Age

Miriam J Johnson
Oxford Brookes
Oxford, UK

ISBN 978-3-031-68133-2      ISBN 978-3-031-68134-9   (eBook)
https://doi.org/10.1007/978-3-031-68134-9

Cover illustration: Pi_Mo_04 Pattern © Melisa Hasan

This Palgrave Macmillan imprint is published by the registered company Springer Nature Switzerland AG.
The registered company address is: Gewerbestrasse 11, 6330 Cham, Switzerland

If disposing of this product, please recycle the paper.

# CONTENTS

CHAPTER 1

# Performing Authorship Online

**Abstract** This chapter provides an overview of the evolving landscape of authorship in the digital age, focusing on how writers perform their roles in online spaces. It considers the construction of digital personas, management of public images, and engagement with readers through social media. Using a mixed-methods approach, including surveys, interviews, and X (Twitter) data analysis, the research highlights the complexities of the performance of authorship. Findings reveal a predominantly positive sentiment in online writing communities, despite varied personal motivations and challenges. The overall study also addresses the digital divide, affecting both authors and audiences, and underscores the importance of authenticity and self-presentation in digitally mediated environments.

**Keywords** Authorship • Digital persona • Performance • Social media • Authors

The proliferation of digital technologies has transformed the landscape of writing and publishing, challenging traditional notions of authorship and calling into question established approaches to what it means to be an author in digitally social spaces. As more and more authors turn to online platforms to establish their presence, interact with readers, and promote their work, it becomes increasingly important to understand how authors navigate the performance of their authorship in digital spaces. This

© The Author(s), under exclusive license to Springer Nature   1
Switzerland AG 2024
M. J. Johnson, *The Digital Pen*,
https://doi.org/10.1007/978-3-031-68134-9_1

includes examining the ways in which digital authors construct their online personas, manage their public image, and engage with readers through social media and other interactive platforms.

In 2023, 59.4% of the global population are active social media users (DataReportal 2023a, 10), and these numbers grow when we consider individual nations such as the UK, 84.4% of the population (DataReportal 2023a, 17), and the US, 72.5% of the population (DataReportal 2023b, 17). Focussing on the UK, we can see that female-identifying individuals use social media more than male-identifying users in similar numbers to the US, at just over 50% female.[1] These predominantly female users are mostly in the age range of 18–44, and as a whole they use it to keep in touch with people (DataReportal 2023c, 55–56).

## The Methodology for This Research

To develop a more holistic view of how authors perform the role of authorship in digitally social spaces, this book draws on both qualitative and quantitative methods. The first area of research focussed on authors and how they perceive their own role as 'author' in digitally social spaces and how they perform this role (or not). The second phase of the research involved analysing data from Twitter to identify sentiment in authorship performance. The branching survey was live from January 2022 to January 2023 and collected demographic data as well as what social platforms they use, how many followers they have, how many people they follow, how much time they spend on social media, if they have more than one account on a social platform, and what genre their most recent book is in.

Once the respondents filled in the key data, the last question related to the genre of their most recent book branched them into a series of questions specific to that genre. The genre-specific questions covered topics such as how they identified themselves as an author of that genre, if they did live events as an author, do they have different audiences on different platforms, do they engage with other authors who write in their area, do they engage with readers of their work, do they watch what they say on social as an 'author', do they get involved with political topics on social, do they censor themselves and their content on social from things which might alienate their audience, and do they feel pressure to be 'falling in

---

[1] In the UK the gender split is 51.6% female and in the US it is 53.9% female (DataReportal 2023, 54).

line' with certain social positions based on their role as an author, among follow-up questions. Forty-one authors chose to take part in the survey. And though this is not a large sample size, it allowed for an in-depth analysis of their responses, which were rich and detailed.

Follow-up interviews were undertaken with those authors who opted in.

To further the understanding of the performance of authorship, additional data analyses were conducted on Twitter. A Python script was written and executed to pull 10,000 tweets with each run with the hashtags #amwriting and #iamwriting from April and May 2023. This resulted in 60,000 tweets with either the #amwriting or #iamwriting hashtags. These tweets were concatenated in a single spreadsheet and each duplicate row and row that began with an RT (retweet) was removed. This left 29,439 tweets with the text, the username, and the time and date the tweet was created in 3 columns.

With these 29,439 tweets as a starting point, the text column was then run through a word counter code which drew out word frequencies in the tweets. The words used most frequently were #amwriting (2114), #writingcommunity (616), writing (261), words (229), #writing (157), #writinglife (102), and write (99). The majority of the terms used most were articles (a, and, the), I (508), my (399), and you (352). Of the 7544 words pulled from the tweets, over 7000 of them were used less than 10 times. This tells us about the specific development of the community and the personal nature of writing with the use of keyword indicators. The focus here was on the performative craft of writing, or to be seen as working with words, evidenced in the word count above and expanded in Chap. 2.

Finally, the 29,439 tweets were analysed using sentiment analysis to get an overall feel as to the positive, negative, or neutral tone of the content of the tweets themselves. This was done using NLTK in combination with VADER (Valence Awareness Dictionary and sEntiment Reasoner) sentiment analysis. VADER is an open-source dictionary that is a rule-based analysis tool specifically attuned to sentiment in social media. Each tweet is scored on a basis of −1 to 1, with 0 being neutral. The breakdown of the sentiment of the tweets can be seen in Fig. 1.1.

The overview of the sentiment analysis of the tweets indicates that there was an overall positive sentiment conveyed in the tweets with only a small percentage being negative or very negative. This tells us that authors who are sharing tweets within these hashtags are doing so in a performatively positive fashion, which is considered more in Chap. 1.

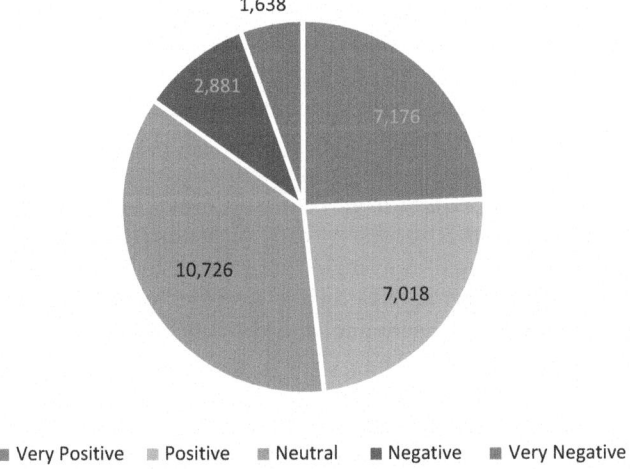

VADER Sentiment analysis of Tweets

1,638

2,881

7,176

10,726

7,018

■ Very Positive   ■ Positive   ■ Neutral   ■ Negative   ■ Very Negative

**Fig. 1.1**   Sentiment analysis of #iamwriting and #amwriting tweets from October 2022 to March 2023

The combination of broad Twitter data with more focused survey and interview data provides a multi-layered analysis. The large dataset from Twitter indicates overall positivity in how authors engage in visible writing communities online. Yet the interviews reveal the more complex motivations and considerations that influence this performance. Authors curate personalities tailored to serve perceived audiences on different platforms.

The mixed methodology utilised in this book incorporates larger data analysis with individual voices to assess both the cultural patterns and personal nuances of the performance of digitally social authorship, part of which is determined at the outset by who has access to and use of social media platforms.

## Access to and Use of Digitally Social Media

One limitation of any study into the use of digital media and technology is the inequality of access to and ability to use social media platforms, newsletters, and online forums to take part in this survey and follow-up interview. Though the phrase 'ease of access' (Seabrooks 2020; Butler

2021) is bandied about in relation to how seemingly universal it is to connect to and make use of digital technologies, these things are often influenced by factors such as age, socio-economic status, social inequality, geographic location, and digital literacy (DiMaggio et al. 2004). It is this 'digital divide' (Van Dijk 2020; Cullen 2001; Lythreatis et al. 2022) that highlights a "division between people who have access and use of digital media and those who do not" (Van Dijk 2020). However, as Van Dijk notes, we should not consider the digital divide as 'has access and uses it' or 'does not', but instead should remain aware that the digital divide is on a spectrum of access and use of digital media. This is something that is highlighted in this study where some authors noted that they find "online interactions difficult and not natural to [them]" while others consider it a necessary part of their brand, another part of their job.

We must also keep in mind that the audiences that these authors seek to reach while performing the role of author in a digital setting are likewise subject to the implications of where they are situated in the spectrum of the digital divide. Both author and audience must work within this framework in order to communicate on social media platforms. Partially echoing the wider patterns of social media use, where Facebook is the most used platform worldwide followed by YouTube and WhatsApp, 80% of authors use Facebook, 77% use WhatsApp (as a form of dark social), and none indicated that they used YouTube to share content. In this study, 75% of authors noted that they use Twitter regularly, whereas worldwide Twitter is much less used. This may be due to the fact that many authors who took part are Western with a wide representation from the US and the UK (who both use Twitter more than the rest of the world).

Of the authors in this study that use social media, the range of followers was vast. The author with the highest number of followers (83,000 on Twitter, 35,000 on Facebook, and 8000 on Instagram) is a self-published author who writes popular fiction. Another author with a small, indie publisher has 31,000 Instagram followers, though their following on Twitter and Facebook are much lower. These high numbers of followers come under Tier 3 content creators, who have a medium reach and a highly engaged audience (Johnson and Simpson 2022, p. 151). For instance, with 31,000 followers on Instagram, a post will reach 2909 users (Statista, 2024a), while a Reel will reach 9,649 (Statista 2024b).

The range of social media follower numbers across the participants were higher than the general user across the three most used platforms, as can be seen in Table 1.1.

**Table 1.1**    Followers for participants vs the average user

|  | *Facebook* | *Instagram* | *Twitter* |
|---|---|---|---|
| Average study author | 3968/520 without outlier | 3778/285 without outlier(s) | 7288/2240 without outlier |
| Average user | 338[a] | 1000–10,000[b] | 159[c] |

[a]On average, n.d.

[b]Mention, 2023

[c]Statista 2022

Table 1.1 highlights that the authors are doing something to boost their follower numbers above those of the general user, this could be directly related to the ways in which they use social media and how they perform themselves and their role as 'author' within those settings. It is interesting to note that though BookTok has over 29.1 billion views (Mcready 2023) and has helped to sell approximately £46m books in 2022 (Kemp-Hadid 2023) that only two of the participants made use of the platform. The participant that uses TikTok most has 2600 followers and writes children's and YA books, which often have an audience that correlates to those of TikTok: predominantly female 18–34 (Kemp-Hadid 2023; Nielsen 2022, p. 31), and it is worth noting that the market for children's and YA books in the UK has a majority female purchasing base, where over 50% of buyers are between 25 and 44 (Nielsen 2022, 32). Likewise, the audience demographics of the platforms more widely play a role in how users and authors interact within and across them.

## So What Is an Author?

Answer: an author is someone who writes something. Or, if we take that romantic idea from Rilke, where if in the still of night you ask yourself: "*must* I write?", and the answer is "I *must*", then you are an author and should "build your life according to this necessity" (Rilke 1962, pp. 18–19).[2] While that harks back to the notion that authorship is something that is inherently within us or not, seeking to define authorship is not a new activity. Questions of authorship, attribution, and authenticity as far back as antiquity and the Renaissance are considered still today (Berardi et al. 2020). Likewise, modern technology and growth of digital

[2] This concept from Rilke was made known in popular culture via Sister Act Two (1993) and is often misquoted as "Don't ask me about being a writer, if when you wake up in the morning and you can think of nothing but writing, then you're a writer".

communities bring to light new questions about authorship in these settings. And, it is here in the digital realm in which this current research is concerned.

Though the concept of 'author' here is more fluid, the role of author is tied to our understanding of what is meant when we say 'book'. Kovač et al.'s (2019) article considering the question of what is a book gives a short overview of how books have been defined by various cultural and governing bodies and suggests updates to the definition, wherein they arrive at the conclusion that a book can be defined as such if it has:

- A minimum length
- Emphasis on the textual content
- Boundaries to its form
- Book information architecture[3] (p. 324)

While this definition seems to offer rigid guidelines on what a book can be, Kovač et al. go on to highlight how these categories of identifiers can stretch across genres, formats, and outputs, which goes some way to aligning with other definitions of a book as content in a variety of containers (Bhaskar 2013) as well as leaving the option open for the potential of sociality in that it can be 'made public' at some stage in its development (Johnson 2021, p. 18).

Using this broad outline of what a book can be, it may be tempting to break up the concept of authorship, as it relates to books, into how an author's books were published. These can be pushed into categories such as self-published, traditionally published, or published in an online setting such as AO3 or Wattpad, among other categories of publication. Furthermore, though authors are writing works on social media platforms, in Twitter feeds, in commentary, and even in reviews, the understanding of a book, here, relates more to those that are made available, or published, in a more formalised manner. That being said, the definition of authorship goes beyond the method of publication. Therefore, while research by Stuart has explored at how authors in traditionally published, self-published, and e-literature sectors present themselves across social media platforms[4] and found that they differed in how they performed the

---

[3] Defined by Kovač et al. as having a title, cover, title page, author, linear structure, and body text [and images] (pp. 322–23, 2019).

[4] Specifically focussing on Twitter and Facebook where Twitter wasn't available, and collecting data a month prior and post book publication.

identity of author, for this particular study the way that authors present themselves as falling into a category of publication format matters less than how they present themselves in digitally social settings as an 'author'—regardless of the output format of their book(s).

A reasonable audience usually agrees that an author is the person who created the work or the person who created the necessary arrangements for the creation of a generated work, in line with the UK's Copyright, Design and Patents Act 1988 (Section 9 [1, 3]). But being an author of a published work in a digitally social space entails a conscious decision to project the identity of 'author' in those spaces; spaces that are part of the consumer's cultural landscape.

The term 'cultural landscape' is a phrase espoused by bodies such as UNESCO as a category of conservation based on physical geographies (Jones 2003), though it has been adopted in other fields of study wherein its symbolic aspects are linked to concepts of power and control of shared information (Rowntree and Conkey 1980). In the field of publishing studies, and more widely in marketing and branding, the cultural landscape takes on aspects of both geography and culture, and the power dynamics those contain. It can be considered as part of the consumer's physical, digital, and theoretical space where they work to align their self-identity and self-projection via the aspects of consumer culture and platforms through which identity is mediated. Though the term 'cultural landscape' is embedded in conservation and geographical studies, we can instead come to see it as being "concerned with all human places and the process of making them and inhabiting them" (Taylor 2012, p. 23). In this sense, the consumer's cultural landscape is a space of performance: both a stage and an audience that continually alter as culture shifts and as we move around the landscape.

With these concepts of the author and the consumer's cultural landscape in mind, this book will consider how authors embody the role of authorship in digital spaces. Chapter 2 will explore how an author identifies and embodies the role of 'author' as it relates to their performance of identity. Here we outline what is meant by 'performance' in relation to an author's self-identity and self-projection drawing on Butler and Loxley's work on performativity as well as Goffman's research into identity as performance, pulling together theatrical concepts and audience studies. Chapter 3 focuses on the concept of authenticity in digitally social settings, what we mean by the term 'authentic', how we can best define its use in online settings, and whether or not it can exist at all in our highly mediated digital environments. Part of the role of authenticity is in guiding authors to perform their concept of self in a 'relatable' or 'real' way, and in doing so they could be tempted to censor themselves to fit into a mould of expectation in order to best align their identity as an 'author' with what they expect the audience to want as they move across the cultural landscape; this is the topic covered in Chap. 4.

## BIBLIOGRAPHY

Berardi, R., Filosa, M., & Massimo, D., 2020. *Defining Authorship, Debating Authenticity: Problems of Authority from Classical Antiquity to the Renaissance.* De Gruyter.

Bhaskar, M., 2013. *The Content Machine: Towards a theory of publishing from the printing press to the digital network.* Anthem Press.

Butler, A. 2021. Ease of Access and Uncomplicated Truth of Social Media: Why critical media literacy is needed (now, more than ever). Media Educational Research Journal. Available at: https://microsites.bournemouth.ac.uk/merj/files/2021/04/9.1-Butler.pdf [Accessed on 09 May 2023].

*Copyright, Design and Patents Act* 1988, 9(1, 3). Available at: https://www.legislation.gov.uk/ukpga/1988/48/part/I/chapter/I/crossheading/authorship-and-ownership-of-copyright.

Cullen, R., 2001. Addressing the digital divide. *Online information review,* 25(5), pp. 311–320.

DataReportal 2023a. Digital 2023: United Kingdom. [Online] Available at: https://datareportal.com/reports/digital-2023-united-kingdom (Accessed: 22 March 2023).

———. 2023b. Digital 2023: United States of America. [Online] Available at: https://datareportal.com/reports/digital-2023-united-states-of-america (Accessed: 22 March 2023).

———. 2023c. Digital 2023: Global Overview Report. [Online] Available at: https://wearesocial.com/uk/blog/2023/01/digital-2023/ (Accessed: 22 March 2023).

DiMaggio, P., Hargittai, E., Celeste, C. and Shafer, S., 2004. Digital inequality: From unequal access to differentiated use. *Social inequality,* pp.355-400.

Johnson, M.J., 2021. *Books and social media: How the digital age is shaping the printed word.* Routledge.

Johnson, M.J. and Simpson, H.A., 2022. *Social Media Marketing for Book Publishers.* Routledge.

Jones, M., 2003. The concept of cultural landscape: discourse and narratives. In *Landscape interfaces: cultural heritage in changing landscapes* (pp. 21–51). Dordrecht: Springer Netherlands.

Kemp-Hadid, A., 2023. TikTok's influence on direct book sales 'relatively small but growing rapidly', says Nielsen. In *The Bookseller* [Online] Available at: https://www.thebookseller.com/news/tiktoks-influence-on-direct-book-sales-relatively-small-but-growing-rapidly-says-nielsen [Accessed 24 March 2023].

Kovač, M., Phillips, A., van der Weel, A. and Wischenbart, R., 2019. What is a Book?. *Publishing research quarterly, 35*, pp. 313–326.

Lythreatis, S., Singh, S.K. and El-Kassar, A.N., 2022. The digital divide: A review and future research agenda. *Technological Forecasting and Social Change, 175*, p. 121359.

Mcready, H., 2023 Everything you need to know about Booktok + 5 best books. [Online] Available at: https://blog.hootsuite.com/booktok/ [Accessed 24 March 2023].

Mention. 2023. Instagram Followers. Mention. Available at: https://mention.com/en/reports/instagram/followers/ [Accessed 24 March 2023].

Nielsen. 2022. UK Book Market in Review 2021. [Online] Available at: https://www.nielsenisbnstore.com/Home/BookScanReport    [Accessed    24 March 2023].

Onaverage.co.uk. n.d. Average Number of Facebook Friends. [online] Available at: https://www.onaverage.co.uk/other-averages/average-number-of-facebook-friends [Accessed 24 Mar. 2023]

Rilke, R.M. 1962. *Letters to a Young Poet.* Translated by M.D. Herter Norton. W.W. Norton & Company, Inc.: New York.

Rowntree, L.B. and Conkey, M.W., 1980. Symbolism and the cultural landscape. *Annals of the Association of American Geographers, 70*(4), pp. 459–474.

Seabrooks, A.D. (2020). Social Media Addiction and Fear of Missing Out: The Moderating Effect of Smartphone Ease of Access.

*Sister Act 2: Back in the Habit.* 1993. Directed by Bill Duke. [Feature film]. US: Touchtone Pictures.

Statista, 2022. Average number of followers and accounts followed by Twitter users in the United States as of May 2021, by tweet volume. Statista Available at https://www-statista-com.oxfordbrookes.idm.oclc.org/statistics/1304702/us-twitter-accounts-followed-and-following-by-tweet-volume/?locale=en [Accessed 24 March 2023].

Statista. 2024a. Average number of users reached per Instagram post from 2023 to 2024, by number of followers. Statista. Available at: https://www.statista.com/statistics/1353274/average-reach-posts-instagram-by-number-of-followers/. [Accessed 16 Setp. 2024].

Statista. 2024b. Average reach of Instagram reels from 2023 to 2024 by number of followers. Statista. Available at: https://www.statista.com/statistics/1356207/instagram-average-reach-for-reels-number-of-followers/. [Accessed 16 Sept. 2024].

Stroud, C., 2004. The performativity of codeswitching. *International Journal of Bilingualism, 8*(2), pp. 145–166.

Stuart, K. 2023. *The Unstable Author Performance: Exploring the 'Innovative' Online Author Identity through Practice-led Research.* PhD thesis. Bangor University.

Taylor, K. 2012. Landscape and meaning. *Managing Cultural Landscapes*, p. 21.

Van Dijk, J., 2020. *The digital divide.* John Wiley & Sons.

# CHAPTER 2

# Identity and Performance of Authorship

**Abstract** Drawing on theoretical frameworks from Goffman, Butler, and Foucault, this chapter explores how authors navigate the complex relationship between their personal identities, their roles as author brands, and the cultural landscapes they inhabit. By focussing on the performative nature of identity, this chapter highlights the fluid and constructed aspects influenced by social norms, cultural expectations, and technological affordances of social media platforms. By analysing survey data, interviews, and social media interactions (on X), we see how authors utilise repetition and ritual in their online performances, engaging with real and imagined audiences to solidify their roles as authors.

**Keywords** Authorship • Performance • Social media • Identity

> *When an individual enters the presence of others, they commonly seek to acquire information about him or to bring into play information about him already possessed [...i]nformation about the individual helps to define the situation, enabling others to know in advance what he will expect of them and what they may expect of him.* (Goffman 1990, p. 13)

When an author publishes a book, regardless of the format, they "need to be on social media" (Lowrey 2022), and, on these connected platforms, authors also need to understand the complex relationship between their

M. J. Johnson, *The Digital Pen*,
https://doi.org/10.1007/978-3-031-68134-9_2

11

role as an author brand, their works, and the way they can navigate the cultural landscape as part of their performance identity as an author. In today's digital age, the role of the author extends beyond the written page. Authors are now expected to cultivate an online presence and connect with readers through social media platforms. How authors construct and perform their identity in these digitally mediated spaces has become an integral part of modern authorship. This involves them managing complex discourses around self-identity, social norms, cultural expectations, and audience engagement. Authors must balance their self-identity and self-projection as their projected persona aims to build their personal brand and resonate with readers.

## What Do We Mean When We Talk About Identity?

For many authors (not all or most, but many), their career as an author is integral to their personal identity. (Fantasy author, 2022)

Though most of us have an understanding of who we are, and what our identity is, it is a term that is almost impossible to pin down and ascribe a widely applicable definition. Identity has been a topic of scholarly inquiry for decades with theorists developing concepts of identity based around works by Freud, Foucault, Butler, Bourdieu, Goffman, and sociological approaches that can take on the questions of how we define, embody, and manipulate identity. Burke and Stets, in their book *Identity Theory*, begin by trying to explain what an identity is in saying that "[a]n identity is the set of meanings that define who one is when one is an occupant of a particular role in society, a member of a particular group, or claims particular characteristics that identify him or her as a unique person" (Burke and Stets 2009). One of the overarching themes that comes through in this, and that of many approaches to identity, is the idea that it is developed and understood in relation to something else. It is not a fixed or inherent characteristic, but rather a fluid and constructed concept influenced by various factors such as social norms and expectations, cultural beliefs, personal experiences, and individual choices. Identity, in this sense, "needs to be understood as not belonging 'within' the individual person, but as produced between persons and within social relations" (Lawler 2021, p. 19). And, therefore, must conform to social constraints that produce an accepted norm.

In the digital realm, there is another layer of algorithmic construct around how an individual, or indeed, an author, can identify in a particular space. Preukschat and Reed note that in these spaces, "[m]ost of what we call 'identity' isn't. It's identifiers. It's how some organization identifies you" (2021). In the case of social media, such as Twitter, Instagram, Threads, Snapchat, or Facebook, which added 56 gender options to their service in 2014 and allows users to choose their preferred pronouns to give choice over how they present (or project) their identity in these spaces,[1] this is evidenced by the platform's structural boundaries that give users the illusion of freedom of choice. The platform's structures, such as its user experience design, still limit how users can identify and present themselves in these spaces via the areas they can post and react, and the content they are allowed to share and engage with. Though users can feel a sense of autonomy in writing content, posting photos, and engaging with others on a social platform, there is a limit to their interactions. For instance, on Facebook, where a reader can engage with a post by their favourite author, write them a comment, or share the author's post, the reader cannot simply give the author a 'thumbs up' or a wacky smiley face without posting it as a comment, as the 'like' function within Facebook and across many platforms often limits the available formats of quick 'liking' to only a few options.

The role of the platform identifiers and how an author uses them enables authors to have a fluid structure in which to develop how they present themselves (their self-projection). Preukschat and Reed allude to this self-projection when they talk of identity as being "how you are known to yourself and others […it is] much more personal and under your control as a self-sovereign human being" (2021). However, this is a simplistic understanding that conceptualises the 'true self' outside of the structures of culture and power that imbue social platforms and their userbases (Lawler 2021).

Power is not always a negative force, nor does it always come from the top down (Foucault 1980): social platforms have the power to decide what are and are not acceptable forms of engagement within their

---

[1] It should be noted that the optionality provided by platforms such as Facebook is not necessarily to empower users to be their authentic self, but instead is monetisable data that can provide a more granular market for advertisers who want to use the platform to reach potential customers.

ecosystems. But often the reporting of violating posts, content, or profiles is down to other users who seek to maintain their own expectations of platform rules and norms that are not always in line with the platforms' actual T&Cs. Hence platforms often offer a reporting feature that includes the option of "I just don't like it"[2] as a reason to report. Likewise, the concept of power is not tied to the repression of acts or thoughts. Instead, it "traverses and produces things, it induces pleasure, forms knowledge, [and] produces discourse" (Foucault 1980, p. 119). In the digitally social arena, specifically that of the author using a social platform to perform the role of author as part of their self-identity and self-projection, the role of power is that of a producer of pleasure and community. For example, if an author goes on Twitter and sets up an account in order to share that they are writing (#amwriting), they just got an agent, signed a book deal, a cover reveal, tour dates, or sold a film adaptation, etc. they are sharing content that brings themselves, and potentially their audiences, joy within a framework of hope labour. Hope labour, here, is under-compensated work done, often in online social production such as posting content and building an audience (Kuehn and Corrigan 2013) in the hopes that future opportunities will materialise, such as larger audiences that will follow the author and potentially buy their books (Mackenzie and McKinlay 2021).

The hope labour of the author's performance in online spaces shifts part of the activities, costs, and risks of marketing their work (at any stage in the writing or publication process) onto the author as a means of a "future-oriented investment" (Kuehn and Corrigan 2013, p. 10). The relationship between the performance of the author as 'author', the hope labour in which they work, the social constructs of their culture, and the productive aspects of the power of the masses to ensure that the author stays within the community norms, that are a general understanding of the rules of conduct and behaviour for an online space (Heitmayer and Schimmelpfennig 2023), helps to develop an author's identity. How authors approach the use of social media platforms is closely tied to how they work within the intersection of these complex discourses, and the performance of their identity is something that is done in conjunction with an audience.

[2] This is the phrasing in Instagram, as of July 2023.

## THE AUDIENCE IS AMONG US

To perform is to have an audience, whether that audience is real or imagined, large or an audience of oneself. Performing in digitally social spaces, therefore, refers to the act of creating and presenting oneself online through various forms of media. This act of performance is often intentional, as individuals may strategically present themselves in a way that reflects their desired projected identity or personal brand. But all performances are inherently subjective and shaped by the context in which they occur, including the context of who makes us their audience. Furthermore, the way that authors present themselves online is always informed by broader cultural expectations of what is acceptable or desirable by one who is an 'author'.

Lawler notes that there is a tendency in the West to separate the concept of *being* an identity from *doing* an identity (2021, p. 116). While being an identity is related to embodying the role of authorship in an authentic way, doing is a performance. What I refer to as self-projection, or an emergent construction of an identity (Bauman 2000), is the author developing a digitally mediated performance of who they believe their audience most expects or wishes them to be. The author, or indeed a reader or other consumer of culture, might see the performance of their role as if wearing a mask,[3] wherein the mask can be "considered a technique of transforming identity" (Pollock 1995, p. 582) for a particular temporal and cultural audience. The drawing in of temporal aspects to a performance are something worth bearing in mind as at different periods of time, different discourses, platforms, and understanding of authorship prevail. Even in a digitally social setting, the performance of authorship is very different on early 2000s Myspace pages in ways that would not be valid as a performance in modern TikTok or the current roller-coaster of Twitter.[4]

The way that authors approach each platform at any given point in time alters based on what they hope to obtain from their engagement and who they believe their audiences are. Some authors use it to develop their academic reach, "in ways which have led directly to a publication"

---

[3] For further reading on the relationship of masks and identity, see Goffman (1990), Doniger (2005), and Strauss (1997).

[4] Though authors' personal websites are beyond the scope of this research, they too are not immune to being a performance of authorship that takes place in a particular space and time and must be considered in context.

(academic/professional author, 2023), while others met their editors in social platform-based writing groups (fiction author, 2023). Another author of fiction said that on social platforms "I aim to come across as professional and competent, likeable, and funny. I make sure I spell correctly. I often reword a comment or post several times to ensure it reads well. I want people to think I am witty, and capable of writing great stories" (2023). This author is working within the intricate interplay of the available discourses of what they believe the constructs of an 'author' are, what the cultural and social expectations the audience might have of someone who calls themselves an author, the constraints of the platforms they are working within, and, importantly, who they believe their audience is.

As "performance implies something performed by someone to someone[, e]very performance demands its audience and its 'outside world'" (Feinberg 2020, p. 334). In the case of the performance of authorship, the author and the spectator interact through a performance that can be both bought into and sold via posts and interactions online but that cannot be completely controlled by either participant (Feinberg 2020). It is often in the best interest of the performer to have control over the situation in which they perform in order to manipulate the audience's reception of them in a way that is sympathetic to the self-projection of identity the author wishes to convey (Goffman 1990).

The complex nature of the discourse that develops from the interplay between the performance and spectating in digitally social spaces is imbued with aspects of self-identity and self-projection, power dynamics, past experiences, and cultural expectations (Jackson 2004). This discourse of performance here is linked closely to Butler's concept of performativity which she states "is a way of naming a power language has to bring about a new situation or to set into motion a set of effects" (Butler 2015, p. 28); in this case, language mediated via social media platforms.

Scholars such as Gould prefer to differentiate between the terms "performance", "performative", and "performativity" where one can isolate the words, the performance of the words, and the fundamental work of the language used (1995). This uncoupling of terminology around the concept of performance enables research into the performance of authorship in digitally social spaces to explore how the performance of a role, and the words used in that performance, can bring that role, or identity, into existence; one that indicates that authors are a "sort of figurehead [... where] now there's almost always an assumption of what an author owes to their audience online" (Children's/YA author, 2023).

Those who are performing the role of 'author' online are often able to separate what Goffman called the 'backstage' area where they can let their guard down, and the 'front' where they perform the role they want to inhabit and be seen to embody (1990). The use of theatrical metaphors works well for face-to-face encounters, but interactions on social media are asynchronous and can both feel like a personal conversation with friends (one to one) or projecting to wider, perhaps unknown, audience (one to many) wherein these "[i]nternet-based performances are mediated and codified [in that] they exist as pixels on a screen" (Pearson 2009).

Social media platforms exist somewhere between the private and the public where "all utterances are performative" (Jagger 2008, p. 66) and based on the way an author projects their identity in those spaces. One fiction author stated that, "I'm always a fiction author [... I tend] to use social media as if I were famous" (2023). If all "people are simultaneously performers and audience members" (Abercrombie and Longhurst 2003, p. 75), then authors must make and remake meaning based on who they expect is sitting in the audience and who is on stage with them at any given point.

When on stage, the performer can adapt their performance based on who makes up their audiences to help to control their audiences' impression of them (Goffman 1990). Even in seemingly inconsequential posts, engagements, or follows, the author as performer must do so in a way that is both part of the performance (I am an author therefore I give talks on my writing process, my favourite books, etc.) and part of a means of inoculating against any performances that may give off the wrong impression to their audience (I write YA Fantasy with a diverse cast, therefore it's not out of the ordinary for me to comment on cancel culture of diverse authors).

Leaving aside the very real stages that authors sometimes find themselves occupying at literary events, on panels or in mass media, the stages of social media reduce non-verbal cues and enhance the role of the imagined audience, which is the "mental conceptualization of the people with whom [...the author is] communicating" (Litt 2012. p. 331). Though the author may know a portion of their audience on social platforms, such as other authors, family, friends, co-workers, etc., there is also the audience they do not know, including the ones they hope to have—future readers. This is an example of the collapse of context[5] that is prevalent in online spaces, where many audiences exist in the same space, the same timeline as the author. Because all writing fictionalizes its readers (Ong 1975) so too does the author choose how to perform the role of authorship by imagining who their most valuable audiences are on the platforms they choose to engage on. Social media "collapses multiple audiences into single contexts" (Marwick and Boyd 2011, p. 1), however the motivation for using particular platforms can be indicative of the audiences that already congregate in that space (Semaan et al. 2015). A digital community's ability to communicate is directly linked to the real or imagined demographics of a particular group.

This can lead to authors performing different roles on different platforms. Some consider using social media platforms as an author as needing to be "somewhat more professional" whereas Twitter "very much feels like a place of work" (fiction author, 2023). This sentiment was echoed by other academic authors who stated that "Twitter felt like the right place to be—it wasn't too personal and could be limited to textual elements which seemed to fit" (2023) and "it's where I like/retweet articles and opinions that mean something to me […] it was somewhere I enjoyed spending time" (2023). Another academic author notes that "Instagram is curated […] whereas Tiktok just shows more real things" (2023), though she does go on to say that "everyone puts on a persona [and] I put more professional content on my LinkedIn […] which I probably don't post on my more personal ones, which is Tiktok and Instagram".

Some authors choose to separate out their performances across platforms based on their real and imagined audiences. In detailing how she used the social media platforms differently, one academic author said:

> For me Facebook is a space for personal engagement with friends (I don't have anyone on there I don't consider a friend in real life); Instagram is more of a 'social media' space for me—it's where I follow people I am interested in rather than know, and where I see the most obvious public relations activities. I use a private setting on Instagram because I post images of my child and family, but I also post images of publications to share with the academic groups I know on there. Twitter is my professional facing platform. It's what I use to engage with other academics and publishers to approach them with collaborations and research/publication ideas. (2023)

---

[5] For further reading on context collapse, see Marwick and Boyd (2011), Davis and Jurgenson (2014), Brandtzaeg and Lüders (2018), Bastos (2021), and Wexler et al. (2018).

It isn't just academic authors who use different platforms in different ways. One author of fiction detailed that they use Facebook as a means to connect to old school friends, ex-colleagues, and real audiences from their lived experience. She went on to clarify that she uses Twitter for political commentary, Instagram first to join real friends, and then later as an author, TikTok for "purely self-promotion purposes", and Mastadon to be herself "and play to an imagined audience".

The value of an imagined audience is in how the author engages based on what they expect that audience wants from them. The way they interact with these different audiences can be seen in the quotes above playing out across platforms, where the users depend on their imagination more than in face-to-face conversations (boyd 2010). In 2016 Litt and Hargittai found that over half of the participants in their research on the composition of imagined audiences on Twitter envisioned their audiences to be 'abstract', or not specifically defined. However, when users did consider a target imagined audience, that audience could be broken down into four areas that are worth loosely defining in relation to the performance of authorship: personal—family, friends; communal—other authors and readers; professional—publishers, editors, reviewers; and phantasmal—famous authors, well-known agents, etc. (Litt and Hargittai 2016).

## THE FEELING OF PERFORMANCE

For each of these different audiences, regardless of the social platform on which they are engaged, the author is taking up a social position. In taking up any social position, either formally (as an author) or informally (in a friendship group), authors are putting on a performative role that brings together cultural expectations and identity. One of the ways that we can get a sense of how authors are performing the role authorship in digitally social spaces is by analysing how they present themselves in the way they engage online. With this in mind, we can look more closely at the way authors tap into existing audiences, such as those who follow and take part in Twitter threads such as #iamwriting and #amwriting. By pulling 60,000 tweets with these hashtags from April and May 2023, we get a snapshot of those who are using these hashtags and those who want to engage with those authors. With nearly 30,000 cleaned tweets, I ran word count analysis to see what the keywords were that were being used. Hashtags #amwriting, #writerslife, #writing, and #writingcommunity were among the most repeated words. The performative nature of these hashtags showcases how the author seeks to tap into a particular, imagined audience that by the nature of the hashtags is part of the communal and perhaps professional ties. 'Writing', 'words', 'book', and 'time' are other words that were written by users who joined in these conversations and, again, places the imagined audience as one of a shared community.

While some of these tweets were written with the professional ties in mind, such as those that share tips on writing and marketing a book, links to agents or editors, etc., many more of them focussed on the performance of writing; tweets like "Revising the novel, same as always. On a tough chapter. After working on it (mostly avoiding it) for a week, my house is clean, but the chapter is still messy. I would gladly scrub the exterior of my house to avoid this chapter today, but it's cold outside. No excuses. #AmWriting" (@TonjaMReynolds 2023) or "That little shiver you get up your spine when you've been revising and revising a little piece, and then suddenly—the words are just right. #amwriting" (@FayeRapoDesPres 2023). These tweets are performative in that they are actively putting on the role of author to show their audiences that they are in the process of writing.

Other tweets are meant to engage with other authors and build ties such as "Without downloading any new images, show me your writing process. #WritingCommunity #amwriting #writersoftwitter" (@ KateAltonWrites 2023). This tweet spun off a short thread of authors replying with amusing images that expressed how they felt about the writing process. More recently, @KateAltonWrites has posted to take part in a similar thread to those in #amwriting territory: #amediting. In this post, in July 2023, @KateAltonWrites posted a photo of a desk, with an open laptop on it, indicating that they are in the process of working through their manuscript, and seeking to share this part of the authorial process with a wider community. Though this post had 21 likes and only 389 impressions within the first 24 hours in which it was published, it highlights the complex development of authorial persona in a digitally social space, that is framed within a cultural context and that of hope labour.

Sentiment analysis of the nearly 30,000 tweets indicated that over half the posts were positive or very positive, which leads to the consideration that those authors who engage with the #iamwriting and #amwriting hashtags often do so within the contexts of the understood social norms of these particular communities, which is mostly positive. If we look further to the breakdown of sentiment in the 7545 words that appeared in the nearly 30,000 tweets, the majority of words were neutral in sentiment

(6684)—writing, stamps, lick, the; while the use of notably positive words (498)—awesome, happy, best, love, freedom—outweighed the negative ones (360)—kill, death, die, drown, anger, sorrow, pain, etc. While the sentiment of tweets and words here may be considered a broad brush approach to analysing the sentiment of a community of engagement, it does begin to indicate how authors feel about performing the role of authorship, and importantly, how that feeling relates to their performance, and the roles they feel expected to take on as an 'author'.

This is backed up in the survey and interviews where the majority of authors were mostly positive about the way they interacted in digitally social settings, saying of social platforms, "I also have always wanted to find a sense of community, and I identify as a writer before all else" (fiction author, 2023). One YA author had positive experiences with their audience when they commented that "Every now and then I get sweet emails telling me how much a person enjoys my work" (2023). Though one author of fiction did note that being an author in an online space is "Largely a waste of time" (2022) and a non-fiction author pointed out that "Every time I walked away from Facebook, I felt worse about humanity"[6] (2023).

The roles in digitally social settings that authors take on form a foundation on which they navigate their social and cultural world (Loxley 2007), wherein 'performative' or 'performativity' encompasses both the outwardly and inwardly facing aspects of performance (Parker and Sedgwick 1995, p. 2). Because an author forms who they are partially through the actions they take in moving towards aligning their self-identities and self-projections, the performance of these actions helps to develop an understanding of what an author is in the wider cultural landscape, which is related to the notions of digital artefacts and discursive representations. This highlights the critically linked elements of performance, identity, and technology in our digitally mediated world (Warschauer and Grimes 2007). Performativity, therefore, is closely related to how authors construct identity through their imagined audience's reception, the rituals of their performance, and their repetition.

---

[6] It's worth noting here that the interviewee did go on to explain that Facebook was a place that was populated by family and a past that they did not want to engage with, which could go some way to explaining the negative impact of using this particular social platform.

## THE RITUALS OF REPETITION

Generally speaking, authors have a ritualistic approach to writing. Whether they must take the dog for a walk first, and then light candles in their home office, or prefer to work in a busy local library, or to a soundtrack of Disney tunes, they draw on repetition of conditions to get in the frame of mind to write. For instance, @GinaBlaxill tweeted, "In my favoured coffee shop and someone is sitting in my favoured seat. While I know the seat doesn't belong to me, my irrational rage levels are high 😊#amwriting" (2023). The repetition, or habitual action, that an author performs, does not develop into a stale approach to writing; instead, it is a "rhythmic repetition of movement which are finely attuned to the different affordances of the material and also of the relationship between the material and the maker" (Ross and Glăveanu 2023).

A ritual here can be understood to be a "predefined sequence of symbolic actions often characterized by formality and repetition" (Brooks et al. 2016, p. 71). Brooks, et al. indicate that these performances are lacking a "direct instrumental purpose" (Brooks et al. 2016, p. 71). However, when we consider the performance of authorship, we see that authors often have purposeful goals in mind for when they post across pen names, share promotional content, or engage with others, all of which underline the ritualistic, repetitive, and performative aspects of performing the role of authorship. It is during the ritualistic process of becoming an author in a digitally social space that an author passes from low (not an author) to high (known as an author) status via a "limbo of statuslessness" (Turner 1995, p. 97), wherein they develop their performance of authorship and how it fits in with their self-identity and self-projection within those spaces.

We can utilise Butler's concept of performativity to frame this repetition and the dynamics that enable 63% of participants in this study to say that they are 'always an author online' regardless of the time of day or the platforms that they use. Where one author of fiction says of using social media, that "[i]t's a branding exercise [...] I aim to come across as professional and competent, likeable, and funny [...] My time on Twitter coincides almost exactly with my time deciding to write professionally, so it very much feels like a place of work to me". While another fiction author felt like they occasionally needed to interact with and be followed by readers, interestingly, this same author notes that they are often prompted to share the "not very exciting" elements of their work, such as an image of themselves editing their writing. They feel pushed to do this by seeing other authors that do similar, performative activities, and repeating it as part of their own ritual of posting online. Because "as we copy an imagined original [...] we do those behaviours over and over again—they become second nature" (Lawler 2021, p. 121). In doing so, the repetition of authorial performance draws together the author's self-identity and self-projection.

There is an aspect of repetition of performance that draws on Butler and Derrida that creates meaning as to what being an 'author' is in these digitally social spaces and how one iterates the language of the performance of authorship (Stroud 2004). One fiction author noted that they are "the same bewildered author everywhere", while another highlighted that they "find online interactions difficult and not natural". The performance that some authors find more difficult than others is not a singular act, but is "a repetition and a ritual" (Butler 2008, p. xv) which is manifest in the person, or author, and is partially of a "culturally sustained temporal duration" (Butler 2008, p. xv) that takes place within a specified location—in this case, the platforms on which the author chooses to have a presence. This indicates that authors who perform the role of 'authorship' in digitally social spaces are actively developing a ritual of performativity within a particular platform, at a particular time, making the performance both "forward-looking and retroactive" (Loxley 2007, p. 100). Repetition creates an expectation, wherein the appearance of the repetition is often taken as truth (Butler 2015), the way that authors perform the role of authorship gives them the power to solidify the identity they want to project as part of their brand.

## The Power of Performance

Power works through its subjects through the process of repetition, wherein the continued performance of a particular self-projection (such as authorship) is refined, renewed, and re-embedded each time it is performed (Jagger 2008). The more an audience sees a particular performance of authorship, the more they are likely to associate the performance with that of an 'author', though each instance of performance is bound temporally, therefore to maintain a position of power via performance, an author must repeat the authorial performance in these spaces. One of the ways that an author can work to embed their authorial identity in such a way is to lean into the performance of power, which allows authors to engage with the power dynamics that are embedded in texts, performances, conversations, the canon, and the boundaries that are drawn around and through these areas of the cultural landscape.

When "action taken is often power exercised" (Galinsky et al. 2003, p. 453) the possession of power can lead to the taking of action (Galinsky et al. 2003). Where power is the ability to control digital resources, such as followers, likes, engagements, etc., those who are able to wield it are less likely to follow in the steps of repetition of others that we see in online settings where one author (possessing or seeming to possess power) posts a photo of their workspace, and then other authors (often with less power in this sphere) follow suit, utilising similar hashtags to embed themselves within a conversation that is potentially happening without them. An example of this is where a fiction author shared, "I'd been sitting at my desk and felt the need to show I was editing, even though it's not very exciting. (Interestingly, that had been prompted by seeing another author share a pic of herself at her desk with a coffee, and I thought, 'Well that's what I'm doing too. I should share it.')" (2023).

With this in mind, we can consider the construction of the self as author in digitally social spaces as a "product of the effects of power" (Jagger 2008, p. 51), which are built from the movement of power in a particular time, cultural landscape, and societal norms. Power, in this sense, is not dictated by the author and is instead given to them in their repeated performance of one who wields power, which in turn, normalises the developed power dynamics—yes, that person calls themselves an author and performs that role in a consistent manner online, therefore we consider them to *be* an author. This is a cyclical process where one who possesses power is more likely to act—whether that is in repeating their performance of authorship, engage as an author with authority, or to seek out new audiences, publications, or expansions of their power (Galinsky et al. 2003).

As the author's brand flows through social networks, embedding their brand into the cultural landscape at a particular moment (Lund et al. 2018), the power that is developed in this movement is a co-creation with their audience. The author continually positions themselves as an 'author', and in doing so they engage with their audience to create value when the audience makes use of the author's books, posts, shares, likes, etc. This co-creation of value hinges on the power invested in the author by the audience, and how the author performs their engagement in return— where different types of engagement (or non-engagement) enforce different power dynamics. Where an audience might expect much engagement from a self-published author, or medium engagement from a mid-list author, they would likely expect little to no engagement from an author who is often atop the bestseller lists. Likewise, it could undermine a best-selling author's power dynamic with their audience if they suddenly began to engage with audiences online in a manner that the audience deems unexpected or beneath them.

## Gender and Performance

The forces of modernisation come to bear on how we understand audiences by moving performances from a simple one where "the person performing accentuates his or her behaviour under the scrutiny of others" (Abercrombie and Longhurst 2003, p. 40) in the form of a theatrical performance to one that encompasses the "performances in everyday life" (Schechner 1988, p. xii). The concept of performance of self (self-projection) is rooted in the work of Judith Butler and her understanding of gender as a performance of self within the confines of the community in which the performance takes place. The online spaces where authors are performing the role of authorship vary in how they are utilised based on the norms operating in that cultural landscape. The roles that authors take on in digitally social spaces fall somewhere in between the theatrical performance, where the setting and the stage separate the audience from the performers, and the everyday occurrences, greetings, and engagements where we perform a version of ourselves according to the context. Within social media, and more widely in society, the contexts in which any performances occur have a gendered element, and this gendering alters the way that performers and audiences interact.

Facebook, Instagram, TikTok, Snapchat, YouTube, Pinterest, and WhatsApp all have a majority female-identifying userbase (DataReportal 2023; Statista 2022), and as such "men and women self-select into socially endorsed gender patterns, as they learn those from observing and socially interacting with others" (Krasnova et al. 2017). Cross and Madson indicate that females tend to depend on others more in their development of their self-concept (Cross and Madson 1997), which relates directly to how female-dominated social spaces are used to develop and maintain relationships, reveal more personal information (Kisilevich et al. 2012; Elm and Sundén 2009), and enhance their image in ways that fit societal expectations of gender roles. This is not to say that all the authors in this study, or more widely, align with the above understandings of how female-identifying users of social networking sites engage with each other and themselves; however it is indicative of the way that users, and authors in particular, perform the role of author in those digitally social settings.

As identity is the doing aspect of performance of authorship, the repetition of such a performance reinforces identity, and based on the cultural norms within a platform at a given time, the gender of an author's identity reflects how they engage in these spaces. Female-identifying authors may choose to utilise social platforms where the audiences are less imagined and more understood, such as Facebook, ties are more likely to be personal ties made up of close family and friends where a 'follow' must be accepted before another user has 'full' access to your account.[7] By engaging in more 'intimate' digitally social spaces, female-identifying authors could be trying to mitigate the potential harassment that is known to effect women more in online spaces[8] (Vogels 2021). This is not to say that female-identifying authors will not use social platforms with an audience that is less known, in fact the surveys and interviews in this study indicate that the majority of authors are taking part across platforms in a way that they see to best boost their concept of authorship. However, it must be noted that performances, including gender and authorship, "bring into effect what they name" (Lawler 2021, p. 129) and can only do so within the societal constraints; which relate to gendered norms of platform interactions.

The ability to use an avatar, or representation of self-online, enables users to represent an aspect, or whole, of their identity in digital spaces. Research indicates[9] that it's not as easy to divorce online and offline gender roles and performances from those online, including how female-identifying users interact with others in digital settings in relation to how they respond to questions, use of honorifics, and emojis (Martey et al. 2014). This, in turn potentially alters the ways in which the gender identify of an author is performed in relation to the gendered expectations of offline, societal interactions. And furthermore, authors who are putting forth themselves, their true, 'authentic' selves, as authors, are more likely to engage in the space in a way that aligns to their offline, gender identity. Which brings up questions around what it means to be authentic, and how an author can perform authenticity in that space.

---

[7] Some platforms allow you to limit what certain people see in relation to your account and profile.

[8] Sixty-one per cent of women say that harassment online is a major problem (Vogels 2021).

[9] See Dunn and Guadagno (2012) and Poncin and Garnier (2012).

## Conclusion

The performance of authorship in digitally social spaces is a complex interplay between identity, cultural expectations, platforms, and audiences. Authors construct who they are as an 'author' through the repeated actions and engagements they undertake online. This repetitive performativity reinforces their desired projected identity and brand. Although authors have some autonomy in crafting this performance, they are ultimately constrained by the sociocultural norms, gender roles, and technological affordances of the platforms they use.

Ultimately, identity lives in the tension between internal conceptions of self (self-identity) and external judgements (reactions to self-projection). Authors construct who they are through repetitive engagement with audiences both real and imagined. No performance can ever fully encapsulate the complexity of identity, but the fragments authors share, filtered through the norms of their sociotechnical stage, cohere into a recognisable pattern of performance, naming themselves as 'author' within that space in a way that an audience can perceive as authentically engaging.

## Bibliography

@TonjaMReynolds, 2023. Revising the novel, same as always. On a tough chapter. After working on it (mostly avoiding it) for a week... [Twitter] 26 April. Available at: https://twitter.com/i/web/status/1651211147377360896 [Accessed on 12 July 2023].

@FayeRapoDesPres, 2023. That little shiver you get up your spine when you've been revising and revising a little piece... [Twitter] 11 April. Available at: https://twitter.com/i/web/status/1645756290709303296 [Accessed on 12 July 2023].

@GinaBlaxill tweeted, 2023. In my favoured coffee shop and someone is sitting in my favoured seat... [Twitter] 2 May. Available at: https://twitter.com/i/web/status/1653319839916720135 [Accessed on 12 July 2023].

@KateAltonWrites, 2023. [Twitter]. 06 April 2023. Avalable at: https://x.com/KateAltonWrites/status/1643873595574177800.

Abercrombie, N., & Longhurst, B., 2003. *Audiences: A Sociological Theory of Performance and Imagination*. SAGE Publications: London.

Bastos, M.T., 2021. From global village to identity tribes: Context collapse and the darkest timeline. *Media and Communication*, 9(3), pp. 16–24.

Bauman, R., 2000. Language, identity, performance. *Pragmatics. Quarterly Publication of the International Pragmatics Association (IPrA)*, 10(1), pp. 1–5.

Brandtzaeg, P.B. and Lüders, M., 2018. Time collapse in social media: extending the context collapse. *Social Media+ Society*, *4*(1), p. 2056305118763349.

Brooks, A.W., Schroeder, J., Risen, J.L., Gino, F., Galinsky, A.D., Norton, M.I. and Schweitzer, M.E., 2016. Don't stop believing: Rituals improve performance by decreasing anxiety. *Organizational Behavior and Human Decision Processes*, *137*, pp. 71–85.

boyd, d. 2010. Social network sites as networked publics: Affordances, dynamics, and implications. In *A networked self* (pp. 47–66). Routledge.

Burke, P. J. and Stets, J. E., 2009. *Identity theory*. Oxford: Oxford University Press.

Butler, J. 2008. *Gender Trouble*. London: Routledge.

———. 2015. *Notes Towards a Performative Theory of Assembly* (Harvard, MA, Harvard University Press).

Cross, S.E. and Madson, L., 1997. Models of the self: self-construals and gender. *Psychological bulletin*, *122*(1), p. 5.

DataReportal, 2023. Digital 2023: United Kingdom. [Online] Available at: https://datareportal.com/reports/digital-2023-united-kingdom (Accessed: 22 March 2023).

Davis, J.L. and Jurgenson, N., 2014. Context collapse: Theorizing context collusions and collisions. *Information, communication & society*, *17*(4), pp. 476–485.

Doniger, W., 2005. *The Woman who Pretended to Be who She Was: Myths of Self-Imitation*. Oxford: Oxford University Press.

Dunn, R. A., & Guadagno, R. E. (2012). My avatar and me—gender and personality predictors of avatar-self discrepancy. Computers in Human Behavior, 28(1), 97–106.

Elm, M.S. and Sundén, J. eds., 2009. *Cyberfeminism in northern lights: Digital media and gender in a Nordic context*. Cambridge Scholars Publishing.

Feinberg, J.G., 2020. Understanding Anti-performance: The performative division of experience and the standpoint of the non-performer. *Performance Philosophy*, *5*(2), pp. 332–348.

Foucault, M., 1980. *Power/Knowledge*, ed. C. Gordon, trans. C. Gordon, L. Marshall, J. Mepham, and K. Soper. Hemel Hempstead: Harvester Wheatsheaf.

Galinsky, A.D., Gruenfeld, D.H. and Magee, J.C., 2003. From power to action. *Journal of personality and social psychology*, *85*(3), p. 453.

Goffman, E. 1990. *The Presentation of Self in Everyday Life*. London: Penguin Books.

Gould, T.,1995. 'The Unhappy Performance'. Edited by A. Parker and E. K. Sedgwick. *Performativity and Performance*. London: Routledge.

Heitmayer, M. and Schimmelpfennig, R., 2023. Netiquette as Digital Social Norms. *International Journal of Human–Computer Interaction*, pp. 1–21.

Jackson, A.Y., 2004. Performativity identified. *Qualitative inquiry*, *10*(5), pp. 673–690.

Jagger, G., 2008. *Judith Butler: sexual politics, social change and the power of the performative.* London: Routledge.

Kisilevich, S., Ang, C.S. and Last, M., 2012. Large-scale analysis of self-disclosure patterns among online social networks users: a Russian context. *Knowledge and information systems, 32,* pp. 609–628.

Krasnova, H., Veltri, N.F., Eling, N. and Buxmann, P., 2017. Why men and women continue to use social networking sites: The role of gender differences. *The Journal of Strategic Information Systems, 26*(4), pp. 261–284.

Kuehn, K. and Corrigan, T.F., 2013. Hope labor: The role of employment prospects in online social production. *The political economy of communication, 1*(1).

Lawler, St. 2021. *Identity: Sociological Perspectives.* 2nd Ed. Cambridge: Polity.

Litt, E., 2012. Knock, knock. Who's there? The imagined audience. *Journal of broadcasting & electronic media, 56*(3), pp. 330–345.

Litt, E. and Hargittai, E., 2016. The imagined audience on social network sites. *Social Media+ Society, 2*(1), pp. 1–12.

Lowrey, S., 2022. Social Media and Indie Authors. In *Publishers Weekly.* Available at: https://www.publishersweekly.com/pw/by-topic/authors/pw-select/article/89578-social-media-and-indie-authors.html/ [Accessed on 30 June 2023].

Loxley, J., 2007. *Performativity.* London: Routledge.

Lund, N.F., Cohen, S.A. and Scarles, C., 2018. The power of social media storytelling in destination branding. *Journal of destination marketing & management, 8,* pp. 271–280.

Mackenzie, E. and McKinlay, A., 2021. Hope labour and the psychic life of cultural work. *human relations, 74*(11), pp. 1841–1863.

Martey, R.M., Stromer-Galley, J., Banks, J., Wu, J. and Consalvo, M., 2014. The strategic female: gender-switching and player behavior in online games. *Information, Communication & Society, 17*(3), pp. 286–300.

Marwick, A.E. and Boyd, D., 2011. I tweet honestly, I tweet passionately: Twitter users, context collapse, and the imagined audience. *New media & society, 13*(1), pp. 114–133.

Ong, W.J., 1975. The writer's audience is always a fiction. *Pmla, 90*(1), pp. 9–21.

Parker, A., & Sedgwick, E. K., 1995. *Performativity and Performance.* London: Routledge.

Pearson, E., 2009. All the World Wide Web's a stage: The performance of identity in online social networks. *First Monday.*

Pollock, D., 1995. Masks and the Semiotics of Identity. *Journal of the Royal Anthropological Institute,* pp. 581–597.

Poncin, I., & Garnier, M. (2012). Avatar identification on a 3D commercial website: Gender issues. Journal of Virtual Worlds Research, 5(3). Retrieved from http://jvwr-ojsutexas.tdl.org/jvwr/index.php/jvwr/article/view/6321/6298

Preukschat, A., Reed, D., 2021. *Self-Sovereign Identity*. Manning Publication. Available at: https://learning.oreilly.com/library/view/self-sovereign-identity/9781617296598/. [Accessed on 06 July 2023].

Ross, W. and Glăveanu, V., 2023. The constraints of habit: craft, repetition, and creativity. *Phenomenology and the Cognitive Sciences*, pp. 1–21.

Schechner, R. 1988. Performance Theory. London: Routledge.

Semaan, B., Faucett, H., Robertson, S., Maruyama, M. and Douglas, S., 2015, February. Navigating imagined audiences: Motivations for participating in the online public sphere. In *Proceedings of the 18th ACM Conference on Computer Supported Cooperative Work & Social Computing* (pp. 1158–1169).

Statista 2022. UK Meta audiences by age and gender. Statista. Available at: https://www-statista-com.oxfordbrookes.idm.oclc.org/statistics/1315413/uk-meta-audiences-by-age-and-gender/ [Accessed 24 March 2023].

Strauss, A.L., 1997. *Mirrors and masks: The search for identity*. Transaction publishers.

Stroud, C., 2004. The performativity of codeswitching. *International Journal of Bilingualism*, 8(2), pp. 145–166.

Turner, V., 1995. *The Ritual process: Structure and Anti-Structure*. New York: Aldine de Gruyer.

Vogels, E., 2021. The State of Online Harassment. Pew Research Center. Available at: https://www.pewresearch.org/internet/2021/01/13/the-state-of-online-harassment/ [Accessed on 15 May 2023].

Warschauer, M. and Grimes, D., 2007. Audience, authorship, and artifact: The emergent semiotics of Web 2.0. *Annual Review of Applied Linguistics*, 27, pp. 1–23.

Wexler, M., Yu, Y. and Bridson, S., 2018. Putting context collapse in context. *Journal of Ideology*, 40(1), p. 3.

CHAPTER 3

# Being Your Authentic Self

**Abstract** Authenticity, a currently trending notion, is examined through the lenses of identity, performance, and cultural expectations. Drawing on theoretical insights, this chapter discusses how authors navigate their self-identity and self-projection to present an authentic persona online. It considers how different social media platforms influence perceptions of authenticity, from the curated aesthetics of Instagram to the 'spontaneous' engagement on TikTok. The links between authenticity and the author brand, as well as the ethical considerations in performing authenticity, matter in how 'authenticity' is perceived among audiences, where there is an ongoing negotiation of authenticity.

**Keywords** Authorship • Authenticity • Performance • Social media • Audience

> The necessity of normativity of ordinary language, therefore, is vulnerable: it is an agreement in signification, an attunement, that depends on our maintaining it in our various communities. (Loxley 2007, p. 35)

Googling 'authenticity' brings up over 471 million hits; 'authentic' brings up over 2.5 billion, while in Google scholar these same terms return 3.8

© The Author(s), under exclusive license to Springer Nature                    31
Switzerland AG 2024
M. J. Johnson, *The Digital Pen*,
https://doi.org/10.1007/978-3-031-68134-9_3

million and 5.3 million results,[1] respectively. There is no shortage of new articles on authenticity and influencer currency, authenticity as a cure to what ails you, or how to pursue it in your day-to-day life. One thing that becomes abundantly clear with this quick digital temperature test is that there is no lack of discussion around the concept of authenticity and being authentic. "People use assumptions about identity, including understandings of race, gender, age, and so forth—to organize their social world and inform their interactions" (Kendall 1998, p. 130), and these assumptions are often based in an implicit understanding of the authenticity (or lack thereof) of a performer, or audience, in a digitally social space.

Authenticity is buzzy and cool. It is something that has been a trend in social media for years, even with the development of fake authenticity (the creation of fake models and influencers[2]) heading up large audiences prepandemic. Post-pandemic, what audiences want from their social media interactions has changed. Users want the people/influencers/brands they follow online to add value to their lives (We Are Social 2023) and to be engaging and aspirational, if not always out of reach, and part of that expectation of value is how authentic the content is. Because we have a "cultural preoccupation with authenticity" (Lawler 2021, p. 117) to be "'acting' [or performing a role in a social environment] is understood to be acting 'inauthentically'" (p. 116). This pulls away from Goffman's considerations of performance, wherein the person is the role they perform as author, not just someone shrugging on the mask, or role, of authorship to fulfil expectations in the theatre of the social.

How can an author be authentic in a space where their self-identity and self-projection are tied to the performance of authorship and to an imagined audience? In order to understand the complex relationship between the author, their performance of authorship, and their 'authentic selves', we must first consider what we mean when we talk about authenticity and being authentic in the cultural landscape, of which social media platforms are a part.

---

[1] Searches done on 14 July 2023.
[2] Such as Miquela with 2.7 million followers on Instagram and digital model Shudu with 239,000 Instagram followers.

## DEFINING AUTHENTICITY

Like identity, authenticity is remarkably hard to pin down into a singular definition. Existing at what Kernis and Goldman call the "limits of language" (p. 284, 2006) concepts of authenticity are not new with the rise of digital technology and date back to the ancient Greek philosophers (p. 284). Currently, most definitions of authenticity draw on some aspects of acting "in accordance with the true self, expressing oneself in ways that are consistent with the inner thoughts and feelings" (Harter 2002, p. 382). This overarching understanding of what authenticity is is further supported by Knoll et al.'s consideration that authenticity has two dimensions: self-awareness and self-expression (2015). These two dimensions explicitly link authenticity to identity, wherein an author, in order to be present and authentic self in digitally social settings, needs to understand how they identify as an author and how they must work to perform that identity. This performance of identity is self-fulfilling in that as the more the role of authorship is performed, the more the author aligns their self-identity and self-projection, and the way it is received by the audience as acceptable or not is related to the perceived authenticity of the performance.

If authenticity is "the unobstructed operation of one's true—or core—self in one's daily enterprises" (Kernis and Goldman 2006, p. 294), and the mediation of social media platforms offers new contexts for "presenting a self that is less than authentic" (Lim et al. 2015), authors can find a balance in performing authentically in a way that will resonate with their imagined audiences by better understanding the fluid meaning of authenticity. Kernis and Goldman (2006) breakdown authenticity into four elements that can be utilised together or stand on their own. These elements are an awareness of their own inner-self and motivations; unbiased processing of self-relevant information, which is a willingness to face and explore one's good and bad qualities without bias; their behaviour, acting in a way that is determined and planned for their goals and desired outcomes; and their relational orientation which is the motivation to communicate in a truthful manner to those around them (Reinecke and Trepte 2014).

Other markers of authenticity on digitally social platforms across studies can be boiled down to whether a user's profile matches their 'offline' persona, how consistent a user's profiles are across accounts, and how spontaneous a user is in their posts and wider engagement (Salisbury and

Pooley 2017). Where digitally mediated authenticity comes into play is that these four elements can be used to loosely define what the authenticity means, but all of the elements are performative, in so much that all posting and engaging on digitally socially platforms is a performance for an imagined audience. The fluid nature of authenticity enables authors to make use of its different definitions and elements in order to perform in a way that is best suited for their audience. Because there is a "normative insistence on the authenticity of identity [this] suggests that identity is held to spring from somewhere 'deep within' us and that, when it does not, there is a problem" (Lawler 2021, p. 136).

To present oneself as an authentic author online is to *be* an author both online and off. The more an author develops an understanding of what elements of authenticity resonate with their audiences, the more they highlight those aspects in their performance, and the more they repeat the performance of authorship in this 'authentic' way, the more they become the role they play. "The more an author seems to reveal, the more authentic they will seem and the more relatable they are to a reader or follower" (Johnson and Simpson 2022, p. 12).

## Authenticity Across Platforms

One survey participant who is YA author considered that "now there's almost always an assumption of what an author owes their audience online. Usually it's access—'who you are, what you do, what do you do, and why should I trust that you can write the book that you've written'" (2023). What this YA author has touched on is performing authority as a form of authenticity—'I am capable of writing this particular book and these are the reasons why'. An author might then go about performing their role of author online in ways that support this underlying theme. Such performances might include sharing links to other authors who write on similar topics, joining in conversations around their authorial topic, sharing positive reviews of their work, and highlighting their validation by the wider industry such as sitting on panels, being interviewed, or taking part in readings or other events.[3] This can lead to social platforms feeling "like a place of work" (non-fiction author, 2023), where authors need to curate their performance for their particular audiences.

---

[3] This is not an exhaustive list and is meant to be indicative of offline performances that support the author's online performance of authorship.

Because "authenticity is not central or static" (Cirucci 2014, p. 149) it can be fluid in how it is performed in different spaces. Salisbury and Pooley found that different platforms claim that they offer an authentic space, in ways that their competitors cannot (Salisbury and Pooley 2017). Different platforms also have different user expectations of authenticity. For instance, Instagram is a curated platform where "[p]eople show what their life is like; but it's not real" (Academic author, 2023). And even within a platform such as Instagram, research indicates that the platform's Stories function enables more "spontaneous self-presentation" (Kreling et al. 2022) and a slightly higher perception of authenticity than a grid post. Facebook (another Meta platform, as are Instagram and WhatsApp, among others) embeds authenticity in their platform structures by situating the platforms as a way to be identified across the web (Haimson and Hoffmann 2016) and as such Facebook enforces authenticities in their requirements for users signing up with and making use of their 'real names' on the platform. This forcing of users to have their real name on show set up the rivalry for authentic spaces amongst platforms (Salisbury and Pooley 2017). And, if we consider more closely the role that being able to link named individuals to the wealth of data in their social accounts, that data becomes hugely valuable to an organisation like Facebook's advertising department.

Within Facebook, the different roles of profile pages, pages, and groups all have different expectations of authenticity, wherein a private profile of an author, such as Stephen King, might only be open to his family and friends who have a different expectation of his performance; both his Stephen King Fan Club Group and his Stephen King Fan Club Page are separate places wherein he has been known to drop in and engage with the fans there, as the author: Stephen King.

Social media marketing expert Helen Simpson noted that the word 'authenticity' "makes a lot of people in my industry grate their teeth. We hate it because everyone says 'I want to be authentic' or 'I want to authentically enter into this conversation'" (Simpson 2023). She goes on to point out that if everyone posted online their authentic selves, it would be incredibly dull. The things that are authentic are everyday life and no one wants to see the basic details of daily life. If an author posted across their social platforms their tasks of making a bed, shopping for groceries, or even sitting on the sofa staring into the abyss, it would not be, usually, of interest. Authenticity, in its true form, can be rather mundane. Conversely, even in posting a comment, image, Reel, video, etc. we are curating the content we share—even in a livestream—based on what an imagined audience expects.

The rise of platforms such as BeReal and TikTok as places of authentic engagement in contrast to the hyper-curated Instagram grid or Pinterest board indicates the staying power of the value that is placed on the perception of authenticity. For instance, BeReal enables users a small, random, window of time in a 24-hour period to take and upload a photo of themselves and what is in front of them (using both the phone's front and back cameras) to link into the company's values of authenticity, spontaneity, and kindness (BeReal 2023). TikTok, likewise, is valued for its authenticity in storytelling, based on videos that feel less curated or filtered than other platforms[4] and taps in to the spontaneity that can be considered as more authentic.

It should be noted, however, that posting content on any social platform is a performance and authenticity in these spaces is part of that performative activity in creating an author's identity within those platforms. On TikTok, "you make the video and you edit it, and you put in filters, and you put in music. Everything that you do is non-authentic" (Simpson 2023). The way that wider users and authors are engaging with social media platforms highlight the subtle and, perhaps, unconscious awareness of this juxtaposition of performance and authenticity, insomuch that trends of engagement are changing in these mediated environments and the boundaries of authenticity are being pushed even further.

## The Edges of Authenticity

The more that users on social platforms seek to appear authentic, the more the term 'authentic', as a descriptor, can lose its meaning. This is exacerbated across channels which, as discussed above, have different expectations of authenticity. Because of this, "[o]n social, extreme behaviour is seen as more authentic" (We Are Social 2023). This is related to research that has found that people on social media prefer to connect with others who hold more extreme view than themselves (Goldenberg et al. 2023). The push to the edges of what is seen as normative within a particular

---

[4] An example of another platform that highlights authenticity is Snapchat, which enables users to upload videos that have a limited number of views on the platform. Because the content is meant to disappear after viewing, users may feel they can present a more authentic self.

community draws on the desire to be seen as standing outside the status quo and embracing spontaneity—even as the definitions of both normal and spontaneous alter. The more unusual behaviour a user exhibits, the more they can be seen as real—pushing the performance of self-projection to the extremes (We Are Social 2023).

As the understanding and perception of authenticity is fluid and has altered with the rise of social platforms that engage with displays of daily life, the consideration of what authenticity looks like in those spaces, within those cultural landscapes, moves from the mundane (a post of author's desk with a cup of coffee), to the vulnerable (a video stream of the author's pristine desk, which pans around to show the messy storage space that takes up the rest of the room), to the chaotic (an author who hires a drone to deliver a manuscript to an agent and live-streams it) (We Are Social 2023). Whereas one academic author in this research indicated that on social media they "just try to keep it real" (2023), other fiction authors said that "Instagram feels like a very strange world where nothing is really real" (2023).

This last sentiment highlights the changing perceptions of authenticity where each edge of the scale from the mundane to the extreme now resonates with audiences as an authentic expression of self, whereas the middle ground—a simple filtered image like might be seen on an Instagram grid—comes across as the least authentic. This is partly to do with how it may feel like the world is falling apart—and social media plays a part in how users perceive this 'decline' in a close and personal setting such as their timelines (Fisher 2022). However, authors do not necessarily need to tap into the extremes of authenticity to engage with and develop their imagined audience; it can be done by staying consistently true to the authorial brand they are building.

With this in mind, audiences now expect their authors and brands to take a stand on wider societal issues. Though many authors are not engaged with negotiating the boundaries of activism, "70% of consumers believe it's important for brands to take a public stand of social and political issues" (sproutsocial 2019). While the normal reading audiences do not often expect their authors to be politically/socially active and loud about it, they do want their author, as a brand, to take a stand on key issues when it arises and to "speak their truth" and be authentic while standing up for something (Garcia 2023) that relates to their brand as an author.

## Authenticity and the Author Brand

While "the reputation of a publishing house is now often based upon its marketing power" (Mourits 2021, pp. 355–6), more and more the "goal is not to present the company as a brand, but the authors as individual brands" (p. 356). The author is only second in the publishing branding hierarchy behind that of the book itself (Johnson and Simpson 2022) and is related closely to the wider narrative around the topic of authorship and genre within the consumer's cultural landscape where there may be questions regarding who has the right or ability to write about a particular subject, whether fictional or not.[5]

When publishing houses get involved with the marketing of the author and their book, they can choose to present author narratives as different from the books they write. An example of this might be where a famous author of Instapoetry is publishing a book in a different genre such as romance. The value of the author brand as an Instapoet may hold more sway in the market than that of the plot of the romance and therefore might be the narrative that is promoted by the marketing team. The author may, or may not, lean into these promotional tactics within their own performance navigating the spaces between their books and imagined audiences. However, Mourits notes that when the narratives of author brand differ too much from the narrative of the book they are trying to promote, it can lack authenticity and audience can react negatively (2021).

Some authors find that their author brand is closely tied to their authentic selves and they are "the most authentic [...they] can be" (academic author, 2023) in those spaces, even if they must remain "really aware of what [...their] platform or [...their] persona appears like to others" (fiction author, 2023). In presenting themselves authentically in digitally social settings, being an author *is* their professional and real brand. The authentic self can be seen "as a source of material value which workers [in this case authors] can leverage to build a reputation" (Whitmer 2019). This reputation is directly related to the value the author places on their self-projection as an author brand and that of the imagined audience. In leveraging their reputation, the author can, hopefully, move into a position of power, gain more followers, sell, and grow their real-estate in the

---

[5] This topic will be covered in depth in Chap. 3 where the role of censorship in the performance of authorship comes into focus.

cultural landscape where recognisable author brands often take up more room in more desirable locations.

Authors already have a personal brand, but they must work to hone it in the digital setting to relate to their imagined audiences in order to create an emotional connection with their audiences, which, in turn, requires the audience to engage in some way (Rangarajan et al. 2017). "After all, a brand is not a product in its own right, but rather is a sign or, even more concretely, an icon that embodies an identity myth" (Van den Braber et al. 2021, p. 11). The myth here is the embodiment of the author's self-projection of who they want to be seen as in the cultural landscapes—in this case 'author'. The building of their personal brand as author does not happen only once the book is published, but begins with the concept of writing and sharing a work with a particular audience in mind and continues across the journey of that book through publication and into the world. While the author themselves are the ones who take a leading role in branding their books (Childress 2017), it is down to how they tell the stories around their writing and themselves in a way that resonates with an audience to reduce their risk in buying a book (Lis and Berz 2011). All of these things come together in order to enable the reader to develop the aforementioned emotional connection with an author, link the author to the concept of 'quality', and ensure that the reader can link the author's voice as a USP (Meyers 2011).

The development of an author brand is a moving target that is temporally positioned in the cultural landscape. It can ebb and flow as the real and imagined audiences come together and disperse around the author's social profile and outputs (be they books, podcasts, posts, etc.). The brand of an author can develop over time and can change as they move around the cultural landscape. Likewise, their brand as an author will ebb and flow in relation to the movement of readers across shared aspects of this cultural landscape, as they draw closer to, and pull away from other landmarks such as different publishers, brands, and other authors. And, sometimes the development of an author brand is a co-creation with their readership within a fandom where characters, stories, and setting move beyond the ownership of a single author.

## THE AUTHENTIC AUTHOR AND FANDOMS

"[A]uthenticity in relation to fandom is historically situated, apt to change and be renegotiated over time, and socially constructed" (McCudden 2011, p. 22). Fandoms have a tendency to exist at the edge of authenticity, pushing the boundaries of the 'accepted canon' into areas that break the rules of the story (Goodman 2015). This pushing of boundaries often incorporates storylines beyond the scope of the published work, can subvert genders and sexualities, and can write socio-political concerns into a story where there were none before.

The development of an active fandom around a work enables an author to cultivate a tangible audience that they can potentially tap into and engage with, though in doing so, they could potentially need to loosen the reins on their works—which many authors are not keen to do.[6] The role of participatory culture (Jenkins 1992), here, is not only related to fans 'filling the gap' in works, nor in only pushing the boundaries of the stories, but also deals with the co-creation of the author's brand identity as it relates to their role as 'creator' of the fandom canon. When an author's work is taken into the realm of fan fiction, it legitimates the role of the 'author' as a god-like figure who has written the core text from which all other texts in the fandom arise. Canon, in this sense, relates to a book or story or media that is indispensable to a group of people (fans), that can be understood within this community to be the 'truth' as an unchangeable base text, and can provide the ingroup with a context through which they read and engage with other related texts (Aichele 2001).

In engaging with a fandom, authors are given a platform to embody their performance of authorship for an audience that cares deeply about their work and seeks to explore its edges in a way that tests the boundaries of what could be possible with characters, settings, etc. Where an author's work, or series of works, is canon in a fandom, "being socialized into [...that] fan community means being policed in relation to communal norms" (Hills 2017). The communal norms in fandoms are often to stay authentic to the canon, which can be interpreted in myriad ways and policed by other fans in comments across AO3, Fanfiction.net, Wattpad,

---

[6] Famously J.R.R. Martin, J.K. Rowling, and Ann Rice all did not condone the creation of fan works based on their stories, worlds, and characters, with Rowling and Rice going so far as to use legal threats to remove/stop fan works. Ironically, this did not stop fans writing stories with their characters, as Harry Potter has over 412,000 stories and 'interview with a vampire' has 700 on Archive of Our Own.

and other fan fiction repositories. Authors can choose to engage with fan fictions, or not, and in doing so they have the power to shape and influence the direction of the fandom, by either endorsing and incorporating fan contributions into their work (more likely seen in platforms such as Wattpad where readers can comment in line, ask questions, and make suggestions) or by setting boundaries and maintaining the integrity of their original story. Authors who choose this route must navigate the delicate balance between maintaining control over their works and embracing the participatory nature of fandoms.

This navigation process poses challenges as it raises questions regarding the extent to which authors should engage with fandom suggestions, boundary-pushing storylines, or alternative interpretations of their work. In the realm of fandom, authors must be particularly conscientious about their performance of authorship compared to when they interact with imagined audiences on broader social platforms, wherein disregarding fan input can alienate loyal readership, hinder potential opportunities, and bring to light complex questions of ethical responsibility in the authentic performance of authorship.

## AUTHENTICITY AND ETHICS IN THE DIGITAL AGE

In the mediated setting of social media, the ability to distinguish the "authentic and inauthentic is highly-context dependent" (Varga 2013) and becomes even more tricky when authenticity is used as an ethical characteristic. If authenticity is being true not only to oneself as you are (self-identity), but also to the self you want to become (self-projection) (Bauer 2017) it can provide the condition for the possibility that one can be a moral agent in a meaningful way (Varga and Guignon 2020). However, it does not necessarily have to align with society's moral imperatives. Living an authentic life, in this sense, does not equate with what we might call a morally good life (Frankfurt 1999).

While we like to consider that most authors perform an ethically responsible version of themselves in digitally social settings, this is not always the case—nor are ethics one-sided. We can look to the ethical debates around authors such as J.K. Rowling's stance on transgender rights, Joanne Harris' opposite stance on the same subject, or Kate Clanchy's descriptions in her books that were deemed racist by some, to get a small taste of the role ethics plays in being perceived to be one's authentic self.[7] Consumers and readers will react to the performance of authorship by these authors regardless of how authentic to themselves they may or may not be.

The complexity of the ethics of authenticity relates to the author making a choice of whether or not to perform their authentic selves, when that authenticity could potentially alienate the audiences they wish to reach. Wholeheartedly engaging with the role of authorship, even if the person in question has not yet written or published a book in any form, does not remove that person's authenticity in calling themselves an author if that is the alignment of their self-identity and self-projection. However it does bring into question the ethical responsibility of the 'author' who autonomously chooses to perform that role with the knowledge of how it might be perceived by an audience. Though this author in question may be able to step back from the situation/stage of social media and understand logically that they have not written or published a book, that does not mean that they can always step back from their desire to *be* an author, which may be their authentic truth where "role playing becomes role taking" (Liedtka 2008, p. 240). The "ideal of authenticity has a particular ethical dimension insofar as gaining knowledge about one's individual authenticity and originality is not valued as an end in itself" (Bauer 2017, p. 578), but is valuable as a means of matching one's "ideal that determines [...their] function" (Guignon 2004, p. 8).

When an author's approach to social media is that they are "proud to be an author but it's the book that's important" (travel writer, 2022), we must look to the ethical boundaries that could potentially arise in promoting their work to their imagined audiences. The role of author is not dissimilar to that of influencer (content creator), in that we can draw parallels between the value of authenticity of content creators as a means of driving their position in the cultural landscape as "consumable brands and entrepreneurial ventures" (Duffy 2017) and that of the goals of an author on social media. The authenticity that content creators perform in digitally social spaces is a mediated authenticity that embodies the tension between

---

[7] This is a small subset of authors who are deemed by the wider media and reading public to hold or have written somewhat controversial views around hot-button topics. It is not indicative of the rightness or wrongness of such views as that is not what is considered in this research. Instead, here, the focus is on the ethics of being authentic to themselves in how they present themselves as 'authors' online.

the audience expectation of spontaneous actions and the performance of self (Enli 2015). With this in mind, Wellman et al. (2020) found that content creator's ethical frameworks are informed by their performance of authenticity and credibility with their audience.

The pressure to be 'authentic' for an author in an online space might push them into performing at the edge of authenticity, and in doing so, it might enhance the role of ethical responsibility of the author by holding them to account within their own individual—authentic—laws which could appear to them as much more serious than if those laws were located outside the author (Ferrara 1998). Small infractions of the author's own rules in relation to their authentic self could provide a ripple effect in their self-identity and self-projection, altering how they interact in the future in the cultural landscape. However, the goalposts of ethics of authenticity are less fixed and more malleable in relation to the temporality, the author's alignment of self-identity and -projection, and the reaction of the audience to the author's performance of authenticity.

Not all authors embrace the performative nature of authenticity in digitally social settings with one YA author saying that, "I do think there's a lot of bullshit (sorry) in how authors present themselves online. Everything has to be the most exciting thing ever!!! but if you are in a private chat or on a private twitter with other authors you see how many people hate their covers or their editors or the industry as a whole" (2023). Another academic author noted that when faced with the task of performing their roles as an author on LinkedIn, indicated that they have "more anxiety" because the real and imagined audiences there are more likely question their authenticity and authority in posting as an author.

## Conclusion

The quest for authenticity is fraught with paradoxes. As authors seek to be true to themselves, they inevitably construct personas shaped by audience expectations. What resonates as authentic evolves across platforms and over time as norms shift. The edges of authenticity are continually pushed as users react to endless curation with a desire for extremes. Yet for all its elusiveness, authenticity remains vital to an author's relationship to themselves and their audiences—both real and imagined. The scripts of social life depend on mutual recognition of identity performances, no matter how fluid. Authors balance inner motivations and outward projections, negotiating their place in the cultural landscape. Through repetition and ritual, they solidify their brand in resonating with readers.

In digitally social spaces within the construct of the ever-shifting cultural landscape, the audiences, either real or imagined, that authors face play a role in developing the author's performance of authorship by accepting or rejecting the authenticity of such a performance. As social norms alter within cultures they do so in digital settings enabling aspects of censorship to encroach, limiting how we can define 'authentic' performances.

## Bibliography

Aichele, G., 2001. *The control of biblical meaning: Canon as semiotic mechanism.* A&C Black.

Bauer, K., 2017. To Be or Not to Be Authentic. in Defence of Authenticity As an Ethical Ideal. *Ethical Theory and Moral Practice: An International Forum,* 20(3), pp. 567–580. https://doi.org/10.1007/s10677-017-9803-4.

BeReal, 2023. Community Standards. [Online]. Available at: https://help.bereal. com/hc/en-us/articles/10268394348317 [Accessed on 20 July 2023].

Childress, C., 2017. *Under the Cover: The Creation, Production, and Reception of a Novel.* Princeton, NJ: Princeton University Press.

Cirucci, A.M., 2014. *The structured self: Authenticity, agency, and anonymity in social networking sites.* Temple University.

Duffy, B. E., 2017. (Not) Getting paid to do what you love: Gender, social media, and aspirational work. New Haven, CT: Yale University Press.

Enli, G. 2015. Mediated authenticity: how the media constructs reality. New York, NY: Peter Lang.

Ferrara, A., 1998. *Reflective authenticity: rethinking the project of modernity.* London: Routledge.

Fisher, M. 2022. Is the World Really Falling Apart, or Does It Just Feel That Way? 12 July 2022. The New York Times. Available at: https://www.nytimes. com/2022/07/12/world/interpreter-world-falling-apart.html. [Accessed on 18 July 2023].

Frankfurt, H.G., 1999. *Necessity, volition, and love.* Cambridge University Press.

Garcia, R. C., 2023. Global Trends Shaping Marketing in 2023. Available at: https://wearesocial.com/uk/blog/2023/01/global-trends-shaping-marketing-in-2023/ [Accessed on 21 July 2023].

Goldenberg, A., Bailey, D., Muric, G., Ferrara, E., Schöne, J., Willer, R., Haplerin, E., and Gross, J., 2023. Attraction to Politically Extreme Users on Social Media. OFS Reprints.

Goodman, L., 2015. Disappointing fans: Fandom, fictional theory, and the death of the author. *The Journal of Popular Culture*, *48*(4), pp. 662–676.

Guignon, C., 2004. *On Being Authentic*. Routledge: London.

Haimson, O.L. and Hoffmann, A.L., 2016. Constructing and enforcing 'authentic' identity online: Facebook, real names, and non-normative identities. *First Monday*.

Harter, S., 2002. Authenticity. In CR Snyder & SJ Lopez (Eds.), Handbook of positive psychology: 382–394. London: Oxford University Press.

Hills, M., 2017. From fan culture/community to the fan world: Possible pathways and ways of having done fandom. *Palabra Clave*, *20*(4), pp. 856–883.

Jenkins, H. 1992. *Textual Poachers: Television Fans & Participatory Culture*. New York and London: Routledge.

Johnson, M.J. and Simpson, H.A., 2022. *Social Media Marketing for Book Publishers*. London: Routledge.

Kendall, L., 1998. Meaning and identity in "cyberspace": The performance of gender, class, and race online. *Symbolic interaction*, *21*(2), pp. 129–153.

Kernis, M.H. and Goldman, B.M., 2006. A multicomponent conceptualization of authenticity: Theory and research. *Advances in Experimental Social Psychology*, *38*, pp. 283–357.

Knoll, M., Meyer, B., Kroemer, N. B., & Schröder-Abé, M., 2015. It takes two to be yourself. Journal of Individual Differences, 36(1), 38–53. https://doi.org/10.1027/1614-0001/a000153

Kreling, R., Meier, A. and Reinecke, L., 2022. Feeling authentic on social media: Subjective authenticity across Instagram stories and posts. *Social Media+ Society*, *8*(1), p. 20563051221086235.

Lawler, St. 2021. *Identity: Sociological Perspectives*. 2nd ed.. Cambridge: Polity.

Liedtka, J., 2008. Strategy making and the search for authenticity. *Journal of Business Ethics*, *80*, pp. 237–248.

Lim, J.S., Nicholson, J., Yang, S.U. and Kim, H.K., 2015. Online authenticity, popularity, and the "Real Me" in a microblogging environment. *Computers in Human Behavior*, *52*, pp. 132–143.

Lis, B. and Berz, J., 2011. Using social media for branding in publishing. *Online Journal of Communication and Media Technologies*, *1*(4), p. 193.

Loxley, J., 2007. *Performativity*. London: Routledge.

McCudden, M.L., 2011. *Degrees of fandom: Authenticity & hierarchy in the age of media convergence* (Doctoral dissertation, University of Kansas).

Meyers, T. The Basics of Author Branding, Blue Moon Communications [Online]. Available: http://www.bluemooncommunications.com/white_papers/author_branding.htm [15 March 2011].

Mourits, B., 2021. In van den Braber, H., Dera, J., Joosten, J. and Steenmeijer, M., eds. *Branding books across the ages: strategies and key concepts in literary Branding* (p. 425). Amsterdam University Press.

Rangarajan, D., Gelb, B.D. and Vandaveer, A., 2017. Strategic personal branding—And how it pays off. *Business Horizons*, 60(5), pp. 657–666.

Reinecke, L. and Trepte, S., 2014. Authenticity and well-being on social network sites: A two-wave longitudinal study on the effects of online authenticity and the positivity bias in SNS communication. *Computers in Human Behavior*, 30, pp. 95–102.

Salisbury, M. and Pooley, J.D., 2017. The# nofilter self: The contest for authenticity among social networking sites, 2002–2016. *Social Sciences*, 6(1), p. 10.

Simpson, H., 2023. Interview with Miriam J Johnson. 2 February 2023.

We Are Social. 2023. Global Trends Shaping Marketing in 2023. 5 January. Available at: https://wearesocial.com/uk/blog/2023/01/global-trends-shaping-marketing-in-2023/ [Accessed on 14 July 2023].

Wellman, M.L., Stoldt, R., Tully, M. and Ekdale, B., 2020. Ethics of authenticity: Social media influencers and the production of sponsored content. *Journal of Media Ethics*, 35(2), pp. 68–82.

Sproutsocial, 2019. stand up/stand aside: Brands Creating Change in the Conscious Consumer Era. Available at: https://sproutsocial.com/insights/data/brands-creating-change/ [Accessed on 24 July 2023].

Van den Braber, H., Dera, J., Joosten, J., Steenmeijer, M., 2021. Introduction. In van den Braber, H., Dera, J., Joosten, J. and Steenmeijer, M., eds. *Branding books across the ages: strategies and key concepts in literary Branding* (p. 425). Amsterdam University Press.

Varga, S., 2013. *Authenticity as an ethical ideal*. Routledge.

Varga, S. and Guignon, C., 2020. Authenticity. Available at: https://plato.stanford.edu/entries/authenticity/ [Accessed on 26 July 2023].

Whitmer, J.M., 2019. You are your brand: Self-branding and the marketization of self. *Sociology Compass*, 13(3), p. e12662.

# CHAPTER 4

# Performing Censorship

**Abstract** Focussing in on how authors can censor themselves in digitally social spaces, this chapter highlights the interplay between external control and self-regulation. Online interactions among authors and readers are influenced by cultural norms, platform guidelines, and individual self-censorship. Within this, there are distinctions between hard censorship, soft censorship, and self-censorship, and how these forms shape the performance of authorship. This chapter also considers the role of algorithmic moderation by social media platforms and the impact of public censorship, where community norms and user reports can suppress voices. Through case studies and examples, the chapter reveals how authors navigate these challenges, often engaging in self-censorship to avoid backlash and maintain their public personas.

**Keywords** Censorship • Self-censorship • Social media • Authors

> Censorship is a knot that binds power and knowledge. (Dović 2008)

Online interactions between groups and individuals in digitally social spaces are influenced by a wide array of internal and external factors that operate with and on each other within the discourse, all of which is intrinsically tied to cultural norms and expectations. Though these interactions can be related to the context of offline factors, those rules of conduct cannot be identically translated into an online setting because of different levels of trust, the lack of physical cues in digital settings, and less commonality in cultural contexts (Heitmayer and Schimmelpfennig 2023). With that in mind, the way that authors and readers interact on social platforms is partially governed by how others on those platforms engage and their behaviour changes depending on their professional context as it relates to the identity they are performing. Sometimes, these changes in behaviour are brought forth by censorship in one of its many guises.

Censorship, here, can be defined broadly as "any control that limits the intended content of any communication" (Phelan 1969) on any platform. Furthermore, we can consider that the role of hard censorship, as those censorship rules enforced in law and punished in a formal fashion, is less seen in western nations, generally; while the push of soft- and self-censorship is more prevalent. Soft censorship can be understood as gatekeeping in the broadest sense—being rejected from publication, having a post removed from a social platform, etc.—while self-censorship is a form of moderation performed on the self where an author might not want to "share very much that could be considered personal" in an online space (fiction author, 2023). In the same vein it is useful to keep in mind the distinction between preliminary and retroactive censorship, where the former is the prevention of publication (in the widest sense of that term) and the latter is a removal of already published content (Dović 2008, p. 168).

Löwstedt notes in his research into fighting censorship that "we are used to opposing censorship with freedom [...] however, the concept of freedom was not necessarily an inclusive one" (2021, p. 10). There are levels of 'freedom' in what can be shared in public spaces, much of which is governed by an interplay of cultural context and the power dynamics of ownership of 'public' spaces, such as governments, media corporations, and social media platforms.

Technology has given everyone a voice,[1] but when "anything can be said by more readily available means than ever before, not everything can be said without fear" (Deflem and Silva 2021, p. 3). While fear may seem like a strong term for monitoring what one says online, this chapter will show how emotions not dissimilar to fear relate to censorship in the way authors perform their roles in these spaces. To do so, the focus will be on key areas that deal with censorship and the performance of authorship.

---

[1] The question of everyone having equality of access to technology is covered in the introduction to this book.

The first will explore what role the social platforms themselves have in moderating the content that is posted, both algorithmically and in the reporting and removal of posts and content. Next we will consider how authors navigate their cultural landscape online by censoring themselves based on community expectations and norms, followed by the pressure of public censorship and what power readers (and wider audiences) have in enforcing particular topics and voices to go unheard. Finally, this chapter draws in on the echoes of voices that occur when silences are enforced and what can be done to push back.

## The Move to Algorithmic Moderation and What We Can/not Say

Social media platforms play a key role in mediating both public and private communication (Cobbe 2021). And, while many would agree that content moderation is valuable in that it makes platforms spaces that adhere to balance, dignity, fairness (Tiktok 2023) in how users post and interact, in reality there is a "small number of politically-unaccountable technology oligarchs [that] exercise state-like censorship powers without any similar limitation" (Langvardt 2018, p. 1358). Because social media companies exist as corporate entities in an increasingly capitalistic society that values growth and individuality, they are able to create their own community guidelines in how their platforms are used by those who opt to sign up. This potentially enables platforms such as those owned by Meta to develop "the most important editorial guide sheet[s] the world has ever created" (Miller, qtd in Solon, 2017).

Regardless of how comprehensive, well-structured, or clear the community guidelines may be, there remain several key issues that platforms must contend with in order to properly implement their own content parameters. These can include the sheer amount of content being created and published on platforms, with over 4.8 billion unique, active social media users worldwide (We Are Social 2023), along with the complexities of nuance in language—multiplied across multiple languages (Cobbe 2021). In addition to these technical considerations, there are other concepts at play around legitimacy and trust in the platform and its authority to moderate content in a fair and transparent manner.

Social media platforms are designed as networked gatekeepers who must moderate these vast quantities of data being published, and in doing so, they have the power to decide what does and does not get published, promoted, or removed. The power that platforms have in deciding what exists on their sites is a form of control "enacted at multiple levels and through differing mechanisms, including platform design, algorithmic moderation, and active moderation of posted content" (West 2017, p. 28). While the design of the platform does play a role in what can and cannot be posted, the focus of this research is on the active censoring of content, as opposed to limitations based on design which relate more to the character limits, and what one can post in a technical sense as opposed to the content of said post.

Social media platforms' algorithms are proprietary information and therefore operate like a black box, which is to say it is almost entirely opaque where they, problematically, "make decisions automatically, even in irrelevant cases" (Castets-Renard 2020, p. 5). The goal of such automated moderation is often to prevent content from being posted, flagging up any key phrases (such as those related to eating disorders which several platforms have specific guidelines around), therefore, catching infringing content before it is live. However, these systems are not guaranteed to work across the board and often rely on tagging content in large databases in order for the algorithms to identify violating content and to learn to identify it in the future.

The way these algorithms flag content and learn how to identify new content really only comes to wider attention when it gets something publicly wrong, such as Facebook removing the well-documented photograph from the Vietnam War featuring a naked girl or removing images of Copenhagen's Little Mermaid statue, both in 2016. While algorithms can identify parts of images as being a nude body, and therefore against community guidelines, there remains questions around how effective such algorithmic moderation is: an issue highlighted by the 2012 campaign of 'free the nipple' where posts featuring female nipples are censored on social media and male nipples are not. Likewise, the prevention of posting content against guidelines is more tenuous when it is done via a livestream, where several serious crimes have been streamed live from platforms.

Beyond the algorithmic moderation of content on social platforms, there are usually large groups of poorly paid humans that must sift through flagged posts. These human content moderators[2] are often poorly paid to

---

[2] There are several studies around the damage to mental health that these workers face as low-paid moderators. See Arsht and Etcovitch (2018), Gerrard (2020), Pinchevski (2023), and Das et al. (2020) (among many others).

make "split second decisions on whether to take down questionable content, applying appropriateness criteria that are often ambiguous and culturally specific" (Arsht and Etcovitch 2018). Even when human moderators are used in conjunction with algorithmic moderation, there needs to be transparency in explaining the 'why' something may or may not be removed from a platform or flagged as breaching guidelines (Suzor et al. 2019). There is a lack of transparency in why some posts are flagged, removed, or simply suppressed in their followers' feeds. The ability for platforms to algorithmically moderate content, perhaps, alters the question of "'what can be said' to 'what will be heard' and 'by whom'" (Riemer and Peter 2021). As the data we post on social platforms, in addition to the data we provide in signing up and our general engagement on the platforms, has become more monetisable for marketing purposes, there are questions raised around how free speech is being affected by either amplifying or suppressing content, such as when users are 'shadowbanned'.

Platforms such as Facebook (and Twitter and Snapchat) have been found to apply "different sets of content moderation 'rules' to 'high-powered' users" (Duffy and Meisner 2023, p. 2). Not only are platforms seemingly allowing different moderation rules for powerful users (politicians, celebrities, etc.), they are also supressing more marginalised voices in the practice of shadowbanning. Shadowbanning is a hard-to-detect form of moderation that is the demoting of content in recommendation algorithms or removing it from the view of everyone but the poster (Savolainen 2022; Leerssen 2023). As visibility often equates to revenue for those who make a living via social platforms, this can be detrimental to their livelihoods. While the majority of authors are not influencers who rely on their social platform for revenue (Sophie Hinchliffe aside), shadowbanning of their posts could still negatively impact their reach as an author and their ability to grow audiences. While many platforms deny that shadowbanning exists—and/or do not engage in conversations around it—users from celebrities who post about contentious topics to pole dancers, body positivity activists, and artists (among others) claim to have had their content shadowbanned, sometimes to the detriment of their overall reach and voice. This format of unofficial censorship or quiet censorship plays a role in how users interact with the platforms and each other. This isn't to say that authors will be posting contentious content all the time or that they are subject to shadowbanning just because their engagement drops or their reach falters, but it does raise questions about what are the limits to the content they can post and will likely lead to more consideration of self-censoring if they write about politics, or erotic content, or even stories that question the status quo.

## PRIVATE CENSORSHIP (SELF)

Though the obvious frameworks of censorship in the cultural landscape are those that come from sources outside of the self (platforms) and supress the publishing of content deemed not in compliance with community guidelines, this is but one part of a duality of censorship (Marlin 1999). The other half of the censorship is the person (or group or entity) being censored. And, while this duality of censorship is considered as composed of two separate parties, wherein one (the censor) acts on the other (the censee), this is not always the case and sometimes the censee and the censor are one and the same.

Self-censorship can be described as what happens when an individual decides not to share information or content with their real or imagined audiences because they believe that there is a cost to posting that content and therefore opt not to post (Bar-Tal 2017). The role of self-censorship can be further broken down into public and private self-censorship wherein the public self-censorship is related to an author choosing not to post content that they know will contravene the community guidelines. Private self-censorship is where the author chooses to not publish certain content or engagement, even though it may conform to the community guidelines.

It is this latter form of private self-censorship which is of most interest to authors who are performing the role of authorship on social media platforms, where 63% of participants paid attention to what they posted on social media and how they engaged based on how they felt they were perceived as an 'author' in that space. One non-fiction author said that as they perform the role of authorship, they realise that by putting on that identity it means "being less personal and less able to post freely" (2023).

This concern with posting freely as an author within their chosen genre came up repeatedly even though 81% of authors in this study chose to engage directly with readers if they were asked questions, while just 6% avoided answering readers altogether. Though most of the participants did not have large social media followings, they often built their follower numbers based on their key real and imagined audiences, such as having Twitter account that is "predominantly book bloggers/readers (mostly

women 40+, and young queer people)" (fiction author, 2023). By culti-
vating followers based on particular interests, authors are more likely to
develop an engaged audience; conversely, if they develop audiences across
a variety of interests—wherein they collapse all their audience contexts
into one, they are less likely to have engagement on their posts (Tafesse
and Wood 2021).

When it comes to posting, 57% of authors in this research suggested
that they always watch what they say on social media, and 21% said that
they did this some of the time, based on how they think it will be received
by their audiences. Where one author said that "it's my job as a children's
author to engage in a way that protects the kids I'm writing for, which
means I'll very readily call people out/swear/talk about politics/etc"
(2023), there is an assumption about who that imagined audience is—perhaps beyond the children who might read their books. A YA author suggested that this relates to a space which "began with very good
intentions—'We're writing for teens, let's make sure they have a safe space
with us'—but is definitely being leveraged by people with bad intentions"
(2023). When it comes to wielding influence and the ability to command
that there is a 'safe space' within an author's social feeds, if the author is
not considered an 'influencer',[3] then their audience is potentially more
likely to trust them (Anthony et al. 2020) when they wade into conversations that other authors might privately self-censor. This is especially likely
when it comes to authors who write about/are authorities on environ-
mental (green orientation) issues (Pittman and Abell 2021).

Some authors feel that there is "almost always an assumption of what
an author owes their audience online" (YA author, 2023), and what this
'something owed' is depends on the performance that the author expects
to give to their real and imagined audiences and how that audience is likely
to react to their performance. Some authors choose to present themselves
"as professional, approachable and not controversial [..., as they] do not
wish to alienate anyone" (thriller author, 2023) and try to be "as honestly
me as possible, with the proviso not to post anything that would likely
offend or alienate the audience" (fantasy author, 2023). This theme holds

[3] Much research has been conduction on how we define an 'influencer' (Yamokoski and
Dubrow 2008; Bakshy et al. 2011; Wei and Meng 2021) and what value they bring to brands
(Hermanda et al. 2019; Jiménez-Castillo and Sánchez-Fernández 2019; Jun and Yi 2020)
and how trustworthy they are on social networks (Singh et al. 2020; Liu et al. 2015;
Alboqami 2023; Hofeditz et al. 2022).

true across participants as 58% check their posts on social platforms to ensure that the content they choose to share will not alienate their audiences. Twenty-three per cent more said that they did this when it suited them.

Part of the private self-censorship that came across in this research is based on how authors are aware of their imagined audiences, but are somewhat wary of mis-identifying their real audiences. Because authors "want[...] to manage how they present[...] themselves to various audiences" (Sleeper et al. 2013) they censor the content they share without the ability to target audiences directly (Sleeper et al. 2013). Therefore they self-censor by learning to "avoid flammable topics" (fantasy author, 2023) or "think carefully about what I post [...] or stick to 'liking' posts I agree with, rather than outwardly saying what I think in my own words" (fiction author, 2023). Das and Kramer echo this when they find that on Facebook "posts are [self-] censored more frequently than comments, with status updates and posts directed at groups censored most frequently" (Das and Kramer 2013, p. 120). When authors are working to solidify their self-identity and self-projection within digitally social spaces, they are less likely to engage in ways that could challenge their performance of authorship or cause backlash.

In light of this, some authors take active steps to avoid being pulled into something that could harm their performance of authorship. Authors in digitally social spaces have shown that they are not only aware of the ways that their posts and content might be received and therefore double check what they write, or self-censor what they plan to post, in order to not alienate parts of their audience, some also qualify this self-censorship as 'not being the right place' to engage in 'contentious' conversations. One author of fantasy fiction in this study spoke to the challenge of not rising to the bait of engaging and their thoughts are worth quoting in full when they say:

> I'll happily get involved in what I consider to be a safe, happy, community of people [...] When it comes to people with terrible opinions about human rights or politics, and the debate comes into my timeline, I have to physically force myself to put my phone down and not engage. I tell myself that social media is not a place for proper debate. I tell myself that getting a reaction from me (or anyone) is the aim and I'm falling for their tactics. I tell myself it's probably a bot. Because what I'm fighting inside, is the urge to stand up and point out the inequality/unfairness/inaccuracy of their comment. My

head knows that social media isn't the place to do that, and as long as I speak out in real life, I can rest easy. But it's hard when I see so many things that incite a reaction. [...Twitter] is the place where I have to force myself not to engage. (2023)

Many authors choose to step away from a conversation and not get involved in order to avoid personal conflicts, frictions, and professional repercussions (Hu and Barradas 2023) that might challenge their performance of authorship or damage their brand. However, avoiding conflict in digitally social settings can potentially lead to an author's audience becoming more polarised (Coscia and Rossi 2022) in a wider "culture of outrage" (YA author, 2023) where readers can wield the power of public censorship.

## Public Censorship

Not to be confused with the public self-censorship mentioned above as one of the two areas of self-censorship, here the role of public censorship relates to the public's willingness to censor particular forms, or themes, of engagement on social media. This willingness to censor is not directly related to the governing rules or regulations of the platforms themselves and instead concerns the community norms and audience expectations. These digital community norms are composed of unwritten guidelines of social expectations and appropriate behaviour and adhere to what a particular audience believes to be normal and appropriate (Lutkenhaus et al. 2023). These norms will shift depending on which platforms and communities the authors engage with, where on one platform they can feel that they are unspoken rules to "understanding the cliquishness/hierarchies of authors online" (fantasy author, 2022), and on another they feel more free to say and engage as they like. An author's understanding of community norms is directly related to the dynamic of their real and imagined audiences and the performance they want to give to each.

While algorithmic classifiers were discussed earlier in the chapter in relation to flagging up 'objectionable' content, the second way that content is often flagged up to moderators on platforms is via reporting by other users of the platform who believe that certain posts/content violates the community standards (Feezell et al. 2023). Flagging up content is a key method used by almost all social media platforms, where platform users can report content that violates the community guidelines in some way.

"It is a complex interplay between users and platforms, humans and algorithms, and the social norms and regulatory structures of social media" (Crawford and Gillespie 2016, p. 411). While some content that is posted is legitimately against community guidelines and should be removed based on those criteria, flagging content is much more nuanced than simply highlighting to the platform that content might breach guidelines, flagging content and asking for it to be removed draws on the social, moral, and political leanings of the users who may choose to flag things that simply they do not agree with, such as images of two women kissing, or a naked statue, etc. Flagging content allows users to participate in the government of the platform and the policing of their own community norms in ways that both authors and readers are aware of in their use of the platforms.

It is this awareness of potential censorship and the ways that it could affect the value of the author's performance—as it relates to potentially growing an audience or positioning themselves as a knowledgeable expert or as a reliable author—that drives some authors to not post content or engage with issues that might be important to them as a person, but harmful to their brand as an author. One academic author indicated that even with topics that matter to them personally, that they "wouldn't just jump in and say, 'hey, this is what I think'. It's not worth it, you get drowned out" (2023), or flagged as inappropriate content.

"The potentially abusive use of reporting undermines its value as a gauge of what the community considers as 'proper' content. Moreover, reporting undesirable content can be a collective act" (Zhao and Chen 2023). This reporting-driven form of public censorship is a form of weaponised content moderation in an attempt to suppress voices and points of view that one does not agree with. This can be seen happening in the world of book-social media where there is a form of piling on authors for their books or personal views, where an author of YA fiction mentioned anecdotally that "A twitter account with 25,000 followers once announced that an author friend of mine was a 'bully,' causing that author to delete her twitter account entirely" (2022). The author goes on to say that "I've since seen screenshots where the accuser admits that she made all the allegations up".

More publicly, this 'cancelling' of authors on social media has affected authors such as J.K. Rowling, Kate Clanchy, Amelie Wen Zhao, and many more.[4] This has led to books being pulled, sales being lost, and the rise of sensitivity readers who are employed to help prevent this sort of public censorship, which often finds its steam in digitally social spaces and grows more widely across the cultural landscape where if an author or content is removed from one platform, it might also be removed from another (Díaz and Hecht-Felella 2021). However, the removal of a contentious profile from one platform, or several of the larger ones, does not always mean they lose their voice. Instead they often move to platforms where moderation policies are more lax or where their particular audiences hold more sway in the governance (Kocher 2021). But for those authors who are publicly censored by their communities on major social platforms, but are not in violation of platform guidelines, they may be subject to the suppression of their voice as part of a spiral of silence.

## AN AUTHOR'S SPIRAL OF SILENCE

When someone feels as if their point of view on an issue is not widely shared among their kinship groups or wider communities, they are less likely to speak up about it (Noelle-Neumann 1974). A PewResearch project in 2014 found that while 86% of Americans were willing to discuss a 'controversial' topic in person, only 42% were willing to do the same on Facebook or Twitter (Hampton et al., Hampton et al. 2014). This is echoed here where one academic author noted that while they would be happy to discuss 'controversial' issues on a panel or in person, they would not post it online where an audience on social media is less likely to listen; where "it's just going to be a barrage of people coming at me, without any dialogue which is going to be helpful. None of that is going to be helpful; none of that is going to be useful" (2023). While this academic author did continue to utilise social media, another fantasy fiction author "soon realised that [...they had] very little of value to offer to social media, and so [...they] disengaged" (2023).

The power of public censorship and the spiral of silence where an author simply stops engaging with anything that might not be in line with popular opinion derives its power "from our social nature, from the

---

[4] It should be noted that this book is less concerned with the validity of 'cancelling' the authors mentioned here and instead is interested in the role cancellation plays as part of the wider discourse of public censorship as it relates to the author's performance of authorship on social media.

willingness of society to threaten isolation in reaction to forbidden opinions and behaviors, and from the individual's fear of isolation" (Noelle-Neumann 2016). The fear felt by authors manifests in the fear of losing connection with their real, imagined, and potential audiences online. It is easier to "not be an arse-hat generally" (academic author, 2023) and to simply only stick to the areas that relate directly to their performance of authorship than to jeopardise the reach they might have, or its relation to their potential sales in the future.

Where some authors are pushed to keep their opinions to themselves online in the spiral of silence, others who find themselves in the majority opinion can be said to get more vocal over time (Matthes 2015). One example of this is the vocal rise of some parts of the LGB community (and some allies) and pressure to remove transgender rights from lesbian, gay, and bi rights. Within the literary and academic communities online, there is much contention around authors Helen Joyce, Julie Bindel, Kathleen Stock, and J.K. Rowling. This has culminated in non-fiction books around the topic of the first three authors and Rowling's fictional work *Troubled Blood* that makes a transwoman the villain of her novel. This is not to say that all the voices pushing an anti-trans agenda in publishing are always loud. In fact, the spiral of silence is tied as much to time as it is to culture. It lasts for a limited period of time, and the balance can change as to who has the more widely accepted right to speak (Noelle-Neumann and Petersen 2004). We can see this happening where reviews of Rowling's book were scathingly negative and often based on her views on trans-rights within the book; likewise the *Los Angeles Review of Books* published a highly negative review of Joyce, Bindel, and Stock's books in July 2023.[5]

As the spiral of silence swings, many authors do choose to stay on the middle-ground route and not speak outside of their brand as author, where some have "been careful about posting anything that would cause a [...social media] pile on, or give me days of grief from trolls" (fiction author, 2023). This tendency for staying neutral when performing as an author in digitally social spaces could enable those loudest voices to rise even higher, and sometimes, as in the case with the controversy over trans-rights, it could be used to promote self-censorship and suppression of marginalised voices. A simple example of this is the For You Page on TikTok, wherein the algorithms suggest content based on what a user has

---

[5] You can find this online at: https://lareviewofbooks.org/article/gender-criticism-versus-gender-abolition-on-three-recent-books-about-gender/.

watched, searched for, or engaged with previously, creating epistemic bubbles, wherein members "lack exposure to relevant information and arguments [...] where other voices are not heard" (Nguyen 2020). The more a user engages with particular content, such as #booktok, the more that content fills their For You Page. The difference between epistemic bubbles and echo chambers, which is the term most often used when discussing narrowed conversations with communities on social platforms, is developed by Nguyen to highlight the passive nature of an epistemic bubble, in this case for the users, and the active suppression of voices and distrust of outside narratives (Nguyen 2020) forms the basis of echo chambers.

The oppressive nature of echo chambers and the spiral of silence have a direct impact on the way that authors perform their role of authorship, where 18% feel that they must fall in line with the wider norms of the industry and 24% feel they sometimes need to. One fiction author went so far as to indicate that "[i]t's commentary on the industry where you have to fall in line" (2022), while a fantasy author noted that they are "under pressure to put on a positive slant on publishing experiences and interactions with readers which [...they] don't necessarily feel" alongside the pressure to express "gratitude, compliance, positivity despite the industry being rather exploitative" (2022).

The publishing industry itself is imbued with power dynamics that are continually playing out in more progressively public spaces online and in media, such as the HarperCollins Union strike in the US. Where the voices of those with the power to publish, who often hold this power due to their position in the discourse, are the same voices that have the authority to replace the workforce in the industry who do not fall in line with the voices that benefit from the spiral of silence. We see this happening when publishers choose to publish books by ethically dubious authors or about events that were scandalous but will sell well to a large, vocal group. While this may produce dividends for publishers, it also can promote the dominance of homogenous perspectives, which, in turn, encourages authors to perform their role of authorship in such a way that it will not harm their chances to pass through the gates of the industry and onto readers' bookshelves.

## Tactics of Resistance

Not all authors are willing to step away from confrontation or be silenced by a louder majority. One fiction author in this study held firm to their beliefs and was not pulled down by the spiral of silence and said of this, "on Twitter certainly – I'd talk about politics (particularly around election time) or injustices or equal rights or online petitions. I felt I could be more open and come down on the side of a debate that I considered to be right. [...] I wasn't concerned about alienating anyone because I was being honest about what I thought was right" (2023). Authors such as this who feel that they are in the right are more likely to break the spiral of silence and speak out (Lasorsa 1991). Likewise, authors who hold strong opinions and are certain of those opinions (Matthes et al. 2010) are more likely to share those opinions regardless of whether or not they are in the minority (Noelle-Neumann 1974).

Some authors find themselves stepping into their voice in direct opposition of the potential silencing they may face, where they "felt [they] had a duty to enlighten people" (fantasy author, 2023) and that even if they know it might alienate their audience that they "decide to do it regardless of knowing it will go down badly" (general fiction author, 2023). While one author of travel books noted that "I quite enjoy friction/criticism [...] I enjoy fighting fire with fire" (2023), and another science fiction author said they created a separate Twitter account where they were "just there to vent and retweet" (2023), there are obvious pockets of resistance from authors who are sure of their convictions and, importantly, make that a part of their authorial performance in these spaces.

That being said, though there are very real reasons for authors to be wary about how they approach their engagements on social media platforms, when/if they post something 'controversial' they are not always going to be immediately run offline or lose followers and potential sales. In fact, if authors can identify their real audiences and find a way to connect with them over perceived similarities, an acceptance of those shared characteristics can mitigate the negative implications of enforced social norms (Armstrong and McAdams 2009), which enforce the spirals of silence.

Other ways that authors break the spiral of silence is in code-switching and using multiple accounts. This has been covered throughout this book and manifests in authors putting on different performances on different platforms in order to be able to use their voice in ways that both enables them to be true to themselves (perhaps in speaking openly with friends on a private social account) and to perform as an author in a way that their real and imagined audiences come to expect based on their public brand and publications. Where one fiction author might feel it is their duty to enlighten people, that same author admits that on Instagram "I steer clear of overt politics (party politics and wider issues)" (2023). The code-switching across platforms enables authors to engage with their real and imagined audiences in ways that are safe for them as a normal user and within their authorial performances.

Authors often have accounts across several social media platforms, and when one platform becomes oppressive (for any number of reasons), or they feel they are unable to perform the role of authorship due to public censorship, trolling, or cancellation, they can migrate and reconvene on a different platform. The most recent example of this is the movement of users (including authors and readers) from Twitter to the federated social platform Mastadon, where the features remained similar to those of Twitter, but where each instance is distributed across servers. Though many users stayed on Twitter, they also set up accounts on this new platform that wasn't solely owned by a large tech company. However, later in the year, when Meta launched Threads (a platform similar to Twitter) people migrated in droves, even though this platform was owned solely by one large company. Some users prefer to push back against big tech and their monopoly on social platforms, and their ability to censor things the platforms deemed 'unacceptable'.

The pushback against community guidelines and high-profile removal of accounts from large platforms such as Facebook and Twitter has resulted in the proliferation of platforms that focus on 'free speech' (Telegram, Truth, Gab, etc.), and in reality often become echo chambers for those who choose to be on them. While this is not a comment on the ethics or morality of platforms and their user bases, it does highlight that authors have the ability to migrate to and from platforms wherein the potential audiences can better align with the performance of authorship they are trying to promote. Resistance to censorship and pushing back against the spiral of silence happen across all points of view and political spectrums and are uniquely tied to a cultural moment in time.

## CONCLUSION

Censorship remains a complex force shaping authorial performance and engagement on social media platforms, and as such authors must navigate external rules enforced by platforms and their algorithms, internal motivations towards private self-censorship, and public pressures that can push for silence. Platform algorithms and content moderation policies hold significant power over what authors can say online. However, these corporate gatekeepers often lack accountability, can easily make mistakes, and potentially stifle creative expression. Due to this, some authors find themselves consciously limiting their own engagement to protect their brand as author and to not alienate their real and potential audiences.

Public censorship can be used to weaponise the reporting of content as inappropriate. 'Cancel culture' and online pile-ons indicate how some audiences work to silence authors they disagree with, even within community guidelines. This ties into the rise of the spiral of silence, wherein marginalised opinions remain unspoken to avoid social isolation. However, resistance among authors does emerge, where some choose to speak out despite potential repercussions. By migrating across platforms and code-switching between accounts, authors can overcome some aspects of censorship. Still, industry pressures to conform highlight systemic inequalities that authors can face when seeking validation by the industry and access to their reading publics, which is slowly being overcome as power hierarchies start to shift with the rise of groups and voices within the industry such as unions and those willing to stand up for what they believe is right.

## BIBLIOGRAPHY

Alboqami, H., 2023. Trust me, I'm an influencer!-Causal recipes for customer trust in artificial intelligence influencers in the retail industry. *Journal of Retailing and Consumer Services, 72*, p. 103242.

Anthony, S., DePinto, C., DiMinno, S., Kahan, L. and Markowitz, D., 2020. Influencer Credibility.

Armstrong, C.L. and McAdams, M.J., 2009. Blogs of information: How gender cues and individual motivations influence perceptions of credibility. *Journal of Computer-Mediated Communication, 14*(3), pp. 435–456.

Arsht, A. and Etcovitch, D., 2018. The human cost of online content moderation. *Harvard Journal of Law and Technology, 2*.

Bakshy, E., Hofman, J.M., Mason, W.A. and Watts, D.J., 2011, February. Identifying influencers on twitter. In *Fourth ACM International Conference on Web Seach and Data Mining (WSDM)* (Vol. 2).

Bar-Tal, D., 2017. Self-censorship as a socio-political-psychological phenomenon: Conception and research. *Political Psychology, 38*, pp. 37–65.

Castets-Renard, C., 2020. Algorithmic content moderation on social media in EU law: Illusion of perfect enforcement. *U. Ill. JL Tech. & Pol'y*, p. 283.

Cobbe, J., 2021. Algorithmic censorship by social platforms: Power and resistance. *Philosophy & Technology, 34*(4), pp. 739–766.

Coscia, M. and Rossi, L., 2022. How minimizing conflicts could lead to polarization on social media: An agent-based model investigation. *PloS one, 17*(1), p. e0263184.

Crawford, K. and Gillespie, T., 2016. What is a flag for? Social media reporting tools and the vocabulary of complaint. *New Media & Society, 18*(3), pp. 410–428.

Das, S. and Kramer, A., 2013. Self-censorship on Facebook. In *Proceedings of the International AAAI Conference on Web and Social Media* (Vol. 7, No. 1, pp. 120–127).

Das, A., Dang, B. and Lease, M., 2020, October. Fast, accurate, and healthier: Interactive blurring helps moderators reduce exposure to harmful content. In *Proceedings of the AAAI Conference on Human Computation and Crowdsourcing* (Vol. 8, pp. 33–42).

Deflem, M., & Silva, D. M. D., 2021. *Media and law: between free speech and censorship*. In Deflem, M. and Silva, D. M. D. (eds). First edn. Bingley, UK: Emerald Publishing Limited (Sociology of crime, law and deviance, volume 26).

Díaz, Á. and Hecht-Felella, L., 2021. Double standards in social media content moderation. *Brennan Center for Justice at New York University School of Law*. https://www.brennancenter.org/our-work/research-reports/double-standards-socialmedia-content-moderation.

Dović, M., 2008. Totalitarian and Post-Totalitarian Censorship: From Hard to Soft?. *Primerjalna književnost, 31*(3).

Duffy, B.E. and Meisner, C., 2023. Platform governance at the margins: Social media creators' experiences with algorithmic (in) visibility. *Media, Culture & Society, 45*(2), pp. 285–304.

Feezell, J.T., Conroy, M., Gomez-Aguinaga, B. and Wagner, J.K., 2023. Who Gets Flagged? An Experiment on Censorship and Bias in Social Media Reporting. *PS: Political Science & Politics, 56*(2), pp. 222–226.

Gerrard, Y., 2020. Behind the screen: Content moderation in the shadows of social media. [Online] Available at: https://jolt.law.harvard.edu/digest/the-human-cost-of-online-content-moderation?onwardjourney=584162_v1. [Accessed on 07 August 2023].

Hampton, K.N., Rainie, H., Lu, W., Dwyer, M., Shin, I. and Purcell, K., 2014. Social media and the 'spiral of silence'.

Heitmayer, M. and Schimmelpfennig, R., 2023. Netiquette as Digital Social Norms. *International Journal of Human–Computer Interaction*, pp. 1–21.

Hermanda, A., Sumarwan, U. and Tinaprillia, N., 2019. The effect of social media influencer on brand image, self-concept, and purchase intention. *Journal of Consumer Sciences*, *4*(2), pp. 76–89.

Hofeditz, L., Nissen, A., Schütte, R. and Mirbabaie, M., 2022. Trust Me, I'm an Influencer!—A Comparison of Perceived Trust in Human and Virtual Influencers.

Hu, W. and Barradas, D., 2023, July. Work in Progress: A Glance at Social Media Self-Censorship in North America. In *2023 IEEE European Symposium on Security and Privacy Workshops (EuroS&PW)* (pp. 609–618). IEEE.

Jiménez-Castillo, D. and Sánchez-Fernández, R., 2019. The role of digital influencers in brand recommendation: Examining their impact on engagement, expected value and purchase intention. *International Journal of Information Management*, *49*, pp. 366–376.

Jun, S. and Yi, J., 2020. What makes followers loyal? The role of influencer interactivity in building influencer brand equity. *Journal of Product & Brand Management*, *29*(6), pp. 803–814.

Kocher, C., 2021. Study shows users banned from social platforms go elsewhere with increased toxicity. *Bing U News*. [online] Available at: https://www.bing-hamton.edu/news/story/3178/study-shows-users-banned-from-social-platforms-go-elsewhere-with-increased-toxicity [Accessed on 4 August 2023].

Langvardt, K., 2018. Regulating online content moderation. *Georgetown Law Journal* 106 (5).

Lasorsa, D. L., 1991. Political Outspokenness: Factors Working against the Spiral of Silence. Journalism Quarterly, 68(1–2), 131 140. https://doi.org/10.1177/107769909106800114

Leerssen, P., 2023. An End to Shadow Banning? Transparency rights in the Digital Services Act between content moderation and curation. *Computer Law & Security Review*, *48*, p. 105790.

Liu, S., Jiang, C., Lin, Z., Ding, Y., Duan, R. and Xu, Z., 2015. Identifying effective influencers based on trust for electronic word-of-mouth marketing: A domain-aware approach. *Information sciences*, *306*, pp. 34–52.

Löwstedt, A., 2021. Fighting censorship: A shift from freedom to diversity. In *Media and law: Between free speech and censorship* (Vol. 26, pp. 9–23).

Lutkenhaus, R.O., McLarnon-Silk, C. and Walker, F., 2023. Norms-Shifting on Social Media: A Review of Strategies to Shift Norms among Adolescents and Young Adults Online. *Review of Communication Research*, *11*, pp. 127–149.

Marlin, R., 1999. The muted bugle: Self-censorship and the press. *Interpretting Self-censorship in Canada*, pp. 290–317.

Matthes, J., 2015. Observing the "spiral" in the spiral of silence. *International Journal of Public Opinion Research*, *27*(2), pp. 155–176.

Matthes, J., Rios Morrison, K. and Schemer, C., 2010. A spiral of silence for some: Attitude certainty and the expression of political minority opinions. *Communication Research*, *37*(6), pp. 774–800.

Miller, C., 2017. Qtd in Solon: To censor or sanction extreme content? Either way, Facebook can't win. In *The Guardian*. 23 May 2017. Available at: https://www.theguardian.com/news/2017/may/22/facebook-moderator-guidelines-extreme-content-analysis [Accessed on 01 August 2023].

Noelle-Neumann, E., 1974. The spiral of silence a theory of public opinion. *Journal of communication*, *24*(2), pp. 43–51.

———., 2016. The theory of public opinion: The concept of the spiral of silence. *Annals of the International Communication Association*, *14*(1), pp. 256–287.

Noelle-Neumann, E., & Petersen, T., 2004. The spiral of silence and the social nature of man. In L. L. Kaid (Ed.), Handbook of political communication research (pp. 339–356). Mahwah, NJ: Erlbaum.

Nguyen, C.T., 2020. Echo chambers and epistemic bubbles. *Episteme*, *17*(2), pp. 141–161.

Phelan, J., 1969. Communications Control: Readings in the Motives and Structures of Censorship.

Pinchevski, A., 2023. Social media's canaries: content moderators between digital labor and mediated trauma. *Media, Culture & Society*, *45*(1), pp. 212–221.

Pittman, M. and Abell, A., 2021. More trust in fewer followers: Diverging effects of popularity metrics and green orientation social media influencers. *Journal of Interactive Marketing*, *56*(1), pp. 70–82.

Riemer, K. and Peter, S., 2021. Algorithmic audiencing: Why we need to rethink free speech on social media. *Journal of Information Technology*, *36*(4), pp. 409–426.

Savolainen, L., 2022. The shadow banning controversy: perceived governance and algorithmic folklore. *Media, Culture & Society*, *44*(6), pp. 1091–1109.

Singh, J., Crisafulli, B. and Xue, M.T., 2020. 'To trust or not to trust': The impact of social media influencers on the reputation of corporate brands in crisis. *Journal of Business Research*, *119*, pp. 464–480.

Sleeper, M., Balebako, R., Das, S., McConahy, A.L., Wiese, J. and Cranor, L.F., 2013, February. The post that wasn't: exploring self-censorship on Facebook. In *Proceedings of the 2013 conference on Computer supported cooperative work* (pp. 793–802).

Suzor, N.P., West, S.M., Quodling, A. and York, J., 2019. What do we mean when we talk about transparency? Toward meaningful transparency in commercial content moderation. *International Journal of Communication*, *13*, p. 18.

Tafesse, W. and Wood, B.P., 2021. Followers' engagement with Instagram influencers: The role of influencers' content and engagement strategy. *Journal of retailing and consumer services*, *58*, p. 102303.

Tiktok, 2023. Community Guidelines. Tiktok. Available at: https://www.tiktok.com/community-guidelines/en/community-principles/. [Accessed on 01 August 2023].

We Are Social, 2023. The Global State of Digital in April 2023. Available at: https://wearesocial.com/uk/blog/2023/04/the-global-state-of-digital-in-april-2023/ [Accessed on 02 August 2023].

Wei, J. and Meng, F., 2021. How opinion distortion appears in super-influencer dominated social network. *Future Generation Computer Systems*, *115*, pp. 542–552.

West, S.M., 2017. Raging against the machine: Network gatekeeping and collective action on social media platforms. *Media and Communication*, *5*(3), pp. 28–36.

Yamokoski, A. and Dubrow, J.K., 2008. How do elites define influence? Personality and respect as sources of social power. *Sociological Focus*, *41*(4), pp. 319–336.

Zhao, A. and Chen, Z., 2023. Let's report our rivals: how Chinese fandoms game content moderation to restrain opposing voices. *Journal of Quantitative Description: Digital Media*, *3*.

# CHAPTER 5

# TL;DR

**Abstract** As a summary, the TL;DR puts emphasis on the dual nature of authorship in digital spaces, highlighting the tension between personal identity and public persona. Authors have to continually navigate social media to balance authenticity with audience expectations, underscoring the importance of maintaining an authentic yet marketable presence.

**Keywords** Authorship • Performance • Authenticity • Social media

> I'm definitely performing as a 'literary' person [...] It also serves as a good reminder to me that writing fiction is a career rather than a slightly bonkers extended hobby, and that these are my colleagues and peers. (fiction author, 2023)

This book has examined the way that authors perform the role of authorship in digitally social spaces, where a fundamental tension lies between how they feel as an 'author' and how they project this sense of authorship to their audiences. As such, it provides a snapshot of ongoing identity negotiations occurring in these digital spaces. In speaking to authors across all genres and publishing formats (from self-publishing to traditional publishing houses) alongside an author survey and sentiment analysis of #iamwriting and #amwriting, three key areas came to the surface: performing the role of author and what that means, how authenticity plays

M. J. Johnson, *The Digital Pen*,
https://doi.org/10.1007/978-3-031-68134-9_5

a part in developing the author's sense of self and connection with their readership, and how authors censor themselves in online spaces to work within the expectations of their real and imagined audiences.

Most authors agree that if they plan to publish a book, they need to be on social media. There are some exceptions, where not being on social media is a part of an author's brand, but for the most part the value of developing a community of readers helps an author understand their performance of authorship, as well as potentially extending their audience and possible sales. Part of being an author on social media is about how that author identifies themselves as such and how they can project that understanding of self to their audience. With this in mind, all authors who go on social platforms 'as an author' create a performance of authorship that they believe will resonate most with their audience. Every time they choose to engage on a platform, they take into account the algorithmic elements of that platform in that it may provide a feeling of having the freedom to post and engage with content as they choose, but all of this is done within strict platform structures that limit and guide what can or cannot be posted and the formatting of these posts.

The performance of authorship that authors often undertake on social media is closely related to the concept of putting on a mask as a "technique of transforming identity" (Pollock 1995, p. 582). Where they can put on a particular mask depending on the platform and the audience they are performing for, because all performances are temporal in nature and closely related to the cultural discourses in which they are set. Things that are acceptable on platforms such as Truth Social are potentially less socially acceptable on Instagram or BeReal. The way that authors approach the platforms they choose to take part in alters depending on what they want to achieve from being on each platform.

Some authors choose to go all-in and be only an author on particular platforms, while on others they only engage with close friends and families so that their performance is less geared to audiences that are imagined. Where social platforms enable a context collapse between audiences, authors find themselves needing to walk a line between being an 'author' for those imagined audiences, sometimes in pursuit of hope labour, and those audiences that are real and tangible to the author. The value in the imagined audiences is in how they help to develop the author's identity and performance of authorship, based on who the author believes is out there, and what they want and expect from this potential audience.

An author's inner sense of self as a writer may not fully align with the carefully crafted persona presented to audiences; however, they can develop their performance of authorship by embedding expectations with repetition. Where 63% of the authors in this research said they are 'always an author online' they do this by approaching social media in ways that are familiar and repeatable for an audience and that embed the authors into their role of authorship. This can be seen in how some authors make taking part in posting in threads such as #amwriting/#iamwriting, or in sharing images of their computers and coffee, or writing spaces as part of their repeated performance: all things that are reiterated in order to guide audiences in drawing connections between the author and their role as Author.

A key way that authors can leverage their performance of authorship on social media is in how authentic they come across to their audiences. Authenticity remains a buzzword in marketing and is hard to define. However, we can consider the concept of authenticity as it connects to self-awareness and self-expression, phrases that are aligned with how an author identifies themselves as an author, and how they project that identity to others. The way they do this can differ across platforms where some authors engage only as an author on Twitter, on Facebook they may share more long-form writing about their days, writing habits, or things that have inspired them. In this way, authors can make use of the structures of the platforms to help them perform in an authentic way.

What we are seeing more, post-pandemic, is the push to the edges of authenticity, where the wilder, more unusual content is what is considered more 'authentic' as the term itself becomes so saturated that it loses its value in setting the user or content apart. This has led to a shift where brands performing their authenticity by taking a stand on social issues, with some authors following suit. When an author finds that their brand as an author is embedded with their authentic selves, they have a wealth of source material to drawn on that can work to develop emotional connections with their audiences, thus encouraging those audiences to engage. However, when an author publishes a book that differs from how they present their 'authentic' selves, audiences take note of this and there can be potential loss of audiences, or wider backlash.

An interesting development at the edge of authenticity is the growth of fandoms. Where the development of an active fandom can potentially enable an author to develop relationships with a highly engaged audience, they may also find that in doing so they must let go of full control of their works—and some authors are less willing than others to do this. Though, those that do engage with fandoms, have the possibility of growing a wider audience for their current and future publications.

The engagement with audiences and the performance of authenticity raise important questions about the ethical complexities around performing an authentic self, if that authenticity is not one that the audience aligns with. We see this happen when authors align themselves with groups that are more polarised, such as anti-trans activists. While the authors might be performing their authenticity, it may be in such a way that alienates readers and wider audiences. Though authors may only want to promote their books that have nothing to do with their personal social or political stances, audiences sometimes have difficulty in separating out the author's authentic self (their social or political views) and their performance of authorship. And, sometimes the authors' sales and contracts can suffer from this.

The quest for authenticity is fraught with pitfalls online, and this can lead to the censorship of voices in these digitally social spaces. Though technology has given everyone a voice, not every voice has the same amount of access or amplification. Though users may think they are free to say and post what they like on social platforms, they are actually operating under the auspices of each platform's community guidelines and terms of use—which they will have read (scrolled through) and ticked a box agreeing to when they signed up. Many platforms utilise a mix of human-driven and AI-driven moderation that is opaque at best and discriminatory at worst. Authors who choose to be on social media often keep in the back of their mind the limits of free speech on these privately owned platforms—where the platforms can decide when something is against their guidelines, potentially limit certain types of content being shared, especially from authors who might work in more niche genres. This can lead to warnings, banning of content outright, and the use of shadowbanning where the authors' content is algorithmically demoted among their followers' feeds.

An awareness of the potential to be banned can lead to authors self-censoring what they post. With private self-censorship, authors choose to not post, share, or engage with content where they feel there will be a cost to such engagement. Authors across this research repeatedly noted that they often thought carefully about how what they posted would be perceived (57%), how they might need to fall in line with their area of the publishing industry, and how they might alienate their readers if they posted something that was not in line with their authorial persona. This leads to authors self-censoring how they interact on social media and their readers, lest they be publicly censored.

Some authors find themselves outside the accepted community norms and paying the cost for it in having their content being flagged up by other users. This happens when the content is often not in violation of the community guidelines, but instead bothers other users and therefore is flagged by them. This flagging allows users to engage with the governing of the platform and gives them a sense of power in controlling what the community norms are within a particular group. This can lead to the 'cancelling' of an author, where they are ostracised based on their stance or content on social, which can potentially spiral out of control and does not always silence the offending voices—which often move to platforms with more lax guidelines.

The potential to be censored online can contribute to the spiral of silence where an author feels their point of view is not widely shared (even if it is correct), and they therefore remain silent. This can lead to authors only choosing to engage with non-contentious areas of authorship, books, and uncontroversial subjects. Though the spiral of silence can move from side to side on a topic (from far right to far left, as an example), many authors feel the safest route is the middle ground, which may not align with their authenticity. And, therefore, may enable cracks to show in their performance of authors that potential authors and readers pick up on.

This is not to say that all authors stay the middle course. In fact, many tactics of resistance have come to the fore where authors are stepping into the fray and standing their ground—something seen more widely with brand activism. They are code-switching across platforms, to be able to exist authentically in a social media setting without the need to perform as an author. They are pushing back against community guidelines and the black boxes of content moderation, and they are leaving historically powerful platforms (Twitter, Facebook, Instagram) and moving more to federated servers that hold less centralised power and enable, potentially, more authentic, less censored performances of authorship.

The key finding of this research is that authors strive to find the 'best' performance of their identity as an author, the current performance that resonates most with audiences is imbued with a sense of authenticity, even when authenticity itself is pushed to an extreme to find meaning. However, authors often choose to not go to the edges of authenticity and instead are keenly aware of the need to censor what they post in order to say the middle ground and not alienate either their real or imagined audiences, as their performance of authorship is directly related to growing the connection with these groups.

# BIBLIOGRAPHY

Pollock, D., 1995. Masks and the Semiotics of Identity. *Journal of the Royal Anthropological Institute*, pp. 581–597.

# INDEX[1]

---

[1] Note: Page numbers followed by 'n' refer to notes.

# GPSR Compliance

*The European Union's (EU) General Product Safety Regulation (GPSR) is a set of rules that requires consumer products to be safe and our obligations to ensure this.*

*If you have any concerns about our products, you can contact us on ProductSafety@springernature.com*

In case Publisher is established outside the EU, the EU authorized representative is:

Springer Nature Customer Service Center GmbH
Europaplatz 3
69115 Heidelberg, Germany

The manufacturer's authorised representative in the EU is Springer
Nature Customer Service Centre GmbH, Europaplatz 3, 69115 Heidelberg,
Germany. If you have any concerns regarding our products, please
contact ProductSafety@springernature.com

Printed and bound by CPI Group (UK) Ltd, Croydon, CR0 4YY
29/04/2026
02099538-0002